Freya: Meeting the Norse Goddess of Magic

Morgan Daimler has gifted us with a well-crafted and engaging introduction to the Goddess Freya. She begins with the ancient legends and names of Freya, then takes us through the lore and associations that have accumulated around the Goddess over the centuries, before bringing us right up to date with how Freya is envisioned today, by modern devotees and in popular culture. Truly a must read for anyone interested in or already working with this powerful and intriguing Goddess.

Ceri Norman, author of, *A Beginner's Guide to Ogham Divination* and *Faerie Stones*

Freya: Meeting the Norse Goddess of Magic is the perfect primer for a deeper relationship with a powerful, complex deity. Daimler offers a concise yet thorough survey of the history, lore, and archaeology surrounding Freya's story. This firm foundation informs and supports chapters covering modern practice and contemporary media depictions. With excellent suggestions for personal practice, devotion, and exploration, this book is a great "starter kit" for those just beginning to hail the Vanadis, the great goddess Freya, in their own practice.

Irene Glasse, co-author of *Blackfeather Mystery School: The Magpie Training*

In writing *Freya: Meeting the Norse Goddess of Magic* Morgan Daimler delights us again with the outstanding level of scholarship and penmanship that have become their signature. Through its clarity, structure, and abundant reference material, *Freya: Meeting the Norse Goddess of Magic* is an easy to consult, go-to resource for all those who seek to understand this goddess - whether in pursuit of academic research or seeking spiritual connection. Morgan Daimler does an excellent job in surveying Freya throughout old and modern lore, debunking the myth of the sex goddess, and diving into the clarification of pre and post Christianization mores that shaped the understanding of Freya and influenced the ways people relate to her. The addition of the author's personal experience with Freya, and the inclusion of practical suggestions about developing a personal connection with the goddess make *Freya: Meeting the Norse Goddess of Magic* a priceless resource for everyone interested in this powerful deity.

Daniela Simina, author of, *Where Fairies Meet: Parallels Between Irish and Romanian Fairy Traditions*

It is refreshing to find so much information on Freya in one place in a readable and relatable book. *Freya: Meeting the Norse Goddess of Magic* is well researched and a book I would teach my students from.

Cat Gina Cole, author of *Psychic Skills for Magic and Witchcraft*

The goddess Freya is often spoken about in pagan ritual, myths, and stories, but what do we really know about this lovely goddess? Morgan Daimler summons the history, magic, and lore of Freya into a delightful and thoughtful guide to her mysteries. She incorporates both old and new ways of working with the goddess that not only inspires, but also gives us the tools to summon the power of Freya in a heartfelt way.

Chris Allaun, author of *Otherworld: Ecstatic Witchcraft for the Spirits of the Land*

Morgan Daimler's new book *Freya: Meeting the Norse Goddess of Magic* is a well-balanced blend of scholarship and personal experience, including original poetry, a guided meditation, and suggestions for connecting with the Vanic goddess. From history and mythology to symbology and modern practices, the author has created a comprehensive introduction that offers readers a solid foundation, as well as resources including a bibliography, from which they will be prepared to further their knowledge of Freya. By the end of this short book, those who began with a passing interest will have gained a deeper understanding of the multi-faceted Norse deity.

M. B. Strang, author of *Arrow's Flight*

I have known Freya. I have read the stories and the Havamal. Now after reading Morgan Daimler's *Freya: Meeting the Norse Goddess of Magic*, I finally feel like I understand Freya. Reading felt like sitting with a personal scholar who broke all the information into manageable, easy to understand bites without losing the integrity and enormity of the information itself.

Deborah A Meyeriecks, author of *Macha and the Medic*

Morgan Daimler's *Freya: Meeting the Norse Goddess of Magic* weaves source material with personal experience to present a detailed introduction to Freya's magic. If you want to invite Freya's strength and power into their life, this book offers myths, associations, and practices (and much more) -- just what you need to start a relationship with this unapologetic goddess.

Irisanya Moon, author of *Norns - Weavers of Fate & Magick*

Morgan Daimler present us with a volume that anyone, with no previous knowledge about Freya, could use as first stepping stone to approach the Goddess. Packed with most of the essentials to start your journey with Freya and opening a door for further research on the right direction.

Ness Bosch, Iberian Shamaness, Priestess, Witch and Independent Researcher. Founder of Path of the Bones

As one would expect of Morgan Daimler, her latest book is well researched and written in a style that is easy to comprehend and digest. Despite being a short introductory book on Freya, it is quite comprehensive, including some interesting personal viewpoints, and it makes a worth-while addition to any personal collection on Norse religion.

Luke Eastwood, author of *The Druid's Primer*

No matter the book Morgan Daimler can always be counted on to be thorough, well researched, and honest in their interpretation of the subject matter. It's something I've always held in high esteem, because knowing you're being guided by someone who values the trust you've placed in them is such a gift. As if that in and of itself wasn't enough, Morgan always manages the difficult task of taking that scholarship and making it approachable. In *Freya: Meeting the Norse Goddess of Magic*, I walked away feeling like I knew that deity in a way I had not before. Due in no small part to Morgan sharing with us a sense of their home altar, personal practices, and even a novel I had never read before. It's not often that I find a book I'd recommend without hesitation, but this is one of those books and I can't sing it's praises enough.

Mortellus, author of *The Bones Fall in a Spiral, An Introduction to Necromancy & the Magic of Death*

Morgan Daimler has crafted a book that is both an excellent overview of and introduction to Freya. At once approachable and informative, this Pagan Portal invites readers regardless of background to come to understand Freya from the sources we have and through their own experiences. If you want to develop a relationship with Freya, this book is an excellent place to start and to nurture your journey with Her.

Sarenth Odinsson, author of *Walking the Worlds: Magic and Religion*

Pagan Portals
Freya

Meeting the Norse Goddess of Magic

Pagan Portals
Freya

Meeting the Norse Goddess of Magic

Morgan Daimler

**MOON
BOOKS**
Winchester, UK
Washington, USA

JOHN HUNT PUBLISHING

First published by Moon Books, 2023
Moon Books is an imprint of John Hunt Publishing Ltd., No. 3 East Street, Alresford
Hampshire SO24 9EE, UK
office@jhpbooks.net
www.johnhuntpublishing.com
www.moon-books.net

For distributor details and how to order please visit the 'Ordering' section on our website.

Text copyright: Morgan Daimler 2022

ISBN: 978 1 80341 002 9
978 1 80341 003 6 (ebook)
Library of Congress Control Number: 2022943429

A CIP catalogue record for this book is available from the British Library.

Design: Lapiz Digital Services

UK: Printed and bound by CPI Group (UK) Ltd, Croydon, CR0 4YY
Printed in North America by CPI GPS partners

We operate a distinctive and ethical publishing philosophy in
all areas of our business, from our global network of authors to
production and worldwide distribution.

Contents

This book is dedicated to my friend Patricia Lafayllve, the first person to really introduce me to Freya and the best Freya's woman I know.

With thanks to my kids, Aries and Terry, for putting up with my singlemindedness while I write.

And with thanks to everyone who helped with modern media suggestions, including Joy, Edain, JD, Patty, Cathy, Jayne, Claire, Ashli, Avery, and Christy.

Author's Note

Pagan Portals is a series whose purpose is to offer people a solid introduction to specific topics. This book is intended to serve as such an introduction to the Norse Goddess, Freya, giving the reader a basic overview of the history, mythology, symbols related to Freya as well as her presence in the modern world. It would be impossible in a book this small to cover any of these topics fully, so what we will do here is aim to touch on each of them in a way that gives readers a grounding in the topic. Those who want to go further can look at the bibliography for suggested further reading and pursue connecting to Freya through those who are devoted to her today.

In writing this book I have tried to find a balance between academic sources and personal experiences. As someone who has been part of the Heathen community for over fifteen years, I want to share my own experience honouring Freya as well as my thoughts based on the way that I have seen other people honouring her, but I also want to provide a strong academic resource for readers. I have tried to include an extensive bibliography and list a selection of other references that could potentially help readers connect to this fascinating Vanic goddess in different ways, both through media and experience.

As with all of my books I am using American Psychological Association (APA) formatting for citations which means that after any quoted or paraphrased material you will see a set of parenthesis containing the author's last name and the date the book was published; this can be cross-referenced in the bibliography if you would like to know the source. I realize not everyone likes this style but I prefer it because I find it the most efficient way to reference sources. I am also including endnotes to help clarify some points within the text.

Readers may also notice a degree of repetition within the text as various points are repeated across the book. This is an intentional choice on my part to help readers better retain the information as studies have shown that repetition in learning material aids retention of information. I realize not all readers prefer this but I think it's important to take this approach given the amount of information we are covering in a relatively short book. I also strongly encourage readers to take notes as they go through the book to help better remember key points and names.

It would be impossible to include everything about Freya in a single book of this size, however, I have tried to include what I consider the most pertinent information. Ideally readers will be interested enough to continue researching and reading more, but if this is the only book on the subject that you read it should still give you a solid basic understanding of who Freya was and is. To accomplish this I am looking at sources spanning both Norse and Germanic cultures, historic and modern, as well as both academic books about Freya and those written by people who may not have a university background but do have a passion for the Goddess. I believe that this wide approach is the only way to get a true understanding of any deity fully in context.

This book by nature will likely tend to focus on a more Heathen perspective, both historic and modern, but it is written for anyone interested in Freya regardless of religion or belief system. I realize that this may be something of a contentious approach because some modern practitioners of pagan faiths like Wicca and Asatru can be a bit antagonistic but I would rather cast a wide net than be overly specific in the audience I write for. I don't think that a person's religion matters as much as the intent with which they approach the Gods and the effort they put into learning about them and connecting to them. So, whether you are a Heathen, Asatruar, Reconstructionist,

Neo-pagan, Wiccan, witch or any other variety of pagan or polytheist this book should still be useful to you. That said, however, my own personal experiences will tend to be framed within aspects of my spirituality as an American Heathen with Reconstructionist tendencies.

Morgan Daimler, July 2022

Introduction

One of the most well-known, if not the most well-known, of the Norse goddesses must surely be Freya. She is a mistress of magic, particularly the kind of magic known as seidhr, and claims half the battle dead. She is known as a goddess of love and of lovers and artwork often depicts her as overtly sexual and very beautiful. Yet who is Freya, really? What do we find when we dig under the veneer of popular culture and Victorian stories? Was Odin really her husband? Is she the goddess of love that modern depictions make her out to be? How similar is the magic she practices to the witchcraft of today?

This short introductory book is intended to illuminate these questions and shed light on who Freya is in the mythology and also in Heathenry today. Or, at least given the relative shortness of this text, to offer a starting place to answer those questions. We will explore what we can find about Freya across the Swedish, Norwegian, and Icelandic sources as well as what we find in modern spiritualities that acknowledge her, and we will look at possible ways for people today to create their own connection to Freya.

Her name is derived from an Old Norse word for lady or woman, which is both indicative of her nature as a pre-eminent goddess and also a source of confusion because it exists as a general term or title; if Freya ever had a distinct personal name[1] it has been lost to time. A modern word related to Freya's name is the German 'frau', woman or wife, which shares the same root (Harper, 2022). Adding to this confusion freya and husfreya were used as terms for human women in different contexts, usually ways that would be translated as lady now. While this shows her wider importance in the culture it also makes her deeper nature more mysterious and harder to gain insight into by looking just at the meaning of her name (or title as the case may be).

Unlike Odin, Thor, and Freyr we have no surviving temples or large statues to Freya but she appears frequently in myths and her popularity is genuinely unquestioned. There are many placenames across Norway and Sweden that translate to something like 'Freya's shrine or temple' showing that even though the actual buildings and evidence for them may not have survived they likely did once exist (Simek, 2007). Bellows describes her as *"the fairest of the goddesses, and the most kindly disposed to mankind, especially to lovers."* (Bellows, 1936, p90). There is also an intriguing passage in the Prose Edda where we are told that Freya goes to great lengths to aid one of her devotees because he has made so many offerings to her that her altar shines like glass, showing us that such a practice was known and that she was thought to be swayed by devotion. Her contemporary popularity during the pre-Christian period can also be seen in a law case found in the Saga of the Icelanders which relates the story of a man outlawed for blasphemy after reciting a poem at the All-Thing where he declared Freya to be a bitch.[2]

Freya appears often in the Norse Eddas, both in an active role and also as a point of contention. In several stories giants tried to force the Aesir to relinquish the sun, moon, and Freya as prizes in various contests and in at least one account a giant stole Thor's famous hammer Mjolnir and would return it only in exchange for Freya's hand in marriage. This demonstrates the pivotal importance of Freya in a wider cosmological sense, although the exact context of that importance has been muddied by time.

Freya's myths and stories can be found across over a thousand years of written and oral material, from the end of the first millennia through the modern day. Although she is described as a goddess who came from outside the Aesir, the Norse gods, she is nonetheless one of – perhaps the – most pivotal of the Norse goddesses and quite possibly the most well-known today. O'Donoghue suggests Freya's importance in the historic culture rests on three things associated with her: ongoing abundance, sexual availability, and fertility. These would all have been greatly desirable qualities which were embodied in the goddess and perhaps available to those who called on her. She is often associated with women and women's issues but it would be more accurate to describe her as a domestic goddess, not of marriage as an institution but of the home and all that was necessary to keep it flourishing, and her devotees would include all people rather than any specific gender.

In Norse mythology there are two groups of Gods, the Aesir and the Vanir, who were once rivals but eventually joined together at least to some degree. Freya is one of the Vanic deities and joined the Aesir, along with her father and brother, after the war between the Vanir and Aesir ended; she is in fact the only clearly named Vanic goddess.[3] While the Aesir re the most well-known and often spoken of Gods of the Norse, the Vanir were a secondary group of gods that were also acknowledged, possibly originally as a separate religious cult, and whose mythology eventually intertwined with the more well-known Aesir. Several scholars, such as Turville-Petre, suggest that the war between the Aesir and Vanir may represent the memory of an older rivalry between different cult groups or pantheons which saw their followers initially clashing before merging. Others reject the idea that the events are pseudohistorical and instead see them entirely as mythic in nature, representing the battle between the agrarian Vanir and the war-like Aesir or between the Vanir as symbols of nature and the Aesir as civilization. And, of course, some choose to simply take the story for what it is, the tale of two groups of gods interacting.

The Vanir are widely viewed as deities of fertility and beings who are more strongly connected to the natural world. Njorð is a deity with sway over the harbour, Freyr over crops and weather, and Freya may represent a principle of propagation or reproduction. As Simek describes it the Vanir are gods associated with good weather, sunshine, rain, helpful winds, successful harvest, and favourable seas, all purviews that pertain to fertility and would be appealing to followers who relied on these things to survive. Simek further suggests their use of female directed Seidhr and acceptance of incest[4] could indicate a matrilineal cult and that along with the wider emphasis on fertility could indicate a social divide between Vanic worshippers as farmers and Aesir worshippers as, initially, nobility. Ellis Davidson, for her part, suggest that the two main hallmarks of Freya's historic worship were likely centred on domestic success – i.e. marriage and childbirth – and seidhr; the first remaining acceptable into the Christian period while the second was vilified.

Despite her origins among the Vanir she is listed by Snorri Sturluson as one of the Asynjur, the goddesses of the Aesir and has a prominent place in Norse mythology. While traces of her worship can be hard to discern, beyond place names connected to her, we have a reference in the Poetic Edda 'Oddrúnargrátr' to Freya being invoked in a prayer along with Frigga and the vaettir after a successful birth and in Hálfs saga ok Hálfsrekka to Freya being prayed to for success in brewing. Freya is not known to be connected to explicit ritual practices, although Turville-Petre does note that the Norwegian 'Historia Norvegiae' discusses a Swedish practice of sacrificing kings to Ceres for successful harvests, and suggests that Ceres in this case should be interpreted in context as Freya. It is possible that some of this scarcity of evidence is due to Freya's outsider status once Christianity took over, where she was often reviled for her sexual openness by the new religion which chose to transfer Freya's previous associations to the Virgin Mary (Näsström,1995). Despite that we do have ample evidence of Freya's position and popularity among the pre-Christian peoples of northern Europe and she has continued to be honoured in modern times by those drawn to her various abilities and qualities.

Chapter 1

Who Is Freya?

Although Freya's stories are notable across the myths, to be discussed in the following chapter, much of what we know about her is shaped by her connections to other gods and by what we can glean from the various names she is called or associated with. This may seem like a roundabout way to begin understanding Freya but in truth it offers us a foundation to build from as we move forward and learn about her. To this end we will begin by looking at the various relationships around Freya that define her in different ways and then the variety of names that Freya is known by across the stories.

Freya's familial relationships are complex and some aspects are debated. In this section we will look at the material we find in the myths as well as some more modern speculation (academic and spiritual) about the beings who are closest to Freya and how they connect to her. Readers should understand that in places there are no firm answers only guesses and it's alright to form your own opinions based on what information we do have.

Freya's father is the harbour god Njorð and it is generally accepted that her mother is Njorð's unnamed sister, although Lindow does suggest that the giantess Skadhi is also an option. This is because the passage in the Gylfaginning that mentions Njorð's two children immediately follows the passage about his marriage and divorce from Skadhi. The other references to Freya's mother, however, leave her unnamed and it is stated elsewhere she was Njorð's sister, which Skadhi was not.

There has been speculation that her mother (and Njorð's sister) might be the goddess Nerthus, although there is no clear evidence of this. Nerthus herself is an obscure deity; Simek suggests that she may have once been paired with Njorð, or could have been a hermaphroditic deity who later came to be viewed exclusively as the male Njorð. While Freya's mother is never named in Norse material – and Njorð's sister is unnamed – the idea that it is Nerthus has nonetheless been accepted by many modern Heathens who choose to treat Njorð and Nerthus as a pair.

Freya's brother is Freyr, a Vanic god with layered associations to fertility and crops. The two are clearly established as siblings across the material and both are considered children of Njorð and an unnamed mother, usually assumed to be his sister. Ellis Davidson states as fact that the two are twins.[5] However, this is found nowhere in the mythology; it has been somewhat accepted among modern heathens though, probably with Ellis Davidson as the source. It is likely that this idea is leaning into Dumézil's theory about tripartite ideology which suggested that society could be divided into three classes each of which correlated to a divine archetype. The third function, productivity, was connected to fertility and was thought to include paired or twin deities. Viewing Freyr and Freya through this lens could lead a person to assume they were twins, even without any support in the source material.

Njorð is said to have had his children with his sister and similarly there is at least one source that claims Freya and Freyr were lovers. Simek suggests that brother-sister unions may have been typical for the Vanir, as it was historically for some royal human dynasties. This idea is further supported in the Lokasenna wherein Loki accuses Freya of having been caught sleeping with Freyr to which Njorð responds that a woman can have a husband and other lovers, only to have Loki say that Njorð himself fathered Freyr on his own sister. While this may be read, of course, as a simple exchange of insults within the text we can also see by the accusations and reactions to them that this was perhaps normative among the Vanir. In the Ynglinga

Saga, where the gods are characterized as humans, we are told that it was a Vanic practice but was outlawed by the Aesir with the implication that the Aesir were more morally upright than the Vanir. Lindow suggests that such incest, while possibly normative among the Vanir, ceased as a practice when Njorð, Freyr, and Freya join the Aesir which may explain why Loki makes a point of referencing it during the Lokasenna – it is an insult not because it was a practice of the Vanir but because it was supposed to have stopped now that they were among the more 'civilized' Aesir.

Simek goes so far as to suggest that Freya and Freyr not only had a relationship but may even possibly have been married, perhaps representing a paired set of deities themselves as Njorð and his sister were. Since their names also represent a pairing, Freya meaning lady and Freyr meaning lord, there could be some weight to this idea although it is not widely accepted as far as I know among modern Heathens. Freya and Freyr are most often paired in the context of siblings not as spouses.

By at least the 10th century Freya is said, in mythology, to be married to a mysterious figure named Oðr who is the father of her daughter Hnoss. Very little is known about Oðr, sometimes also called Od, except that he travelled often and that Freya would weep tears of gold in his absence and searched for him while in disguise. The story of Freya and her missing husband would have been one that was highly relatable to people – especially women – of the Viking age who often saw their husbands travelling out for years at a time or being lost at sea altogether (Guðmundsson, 2016). This is worth noting as many modern interpretations of the relationship between Freya and Oðr do not emphasize the context his disappearance may have had to the original audience, yet that context likely was a key aspect of the older story. In this case we might argue that Freya is not a goddess who is abandoned by an unloving spouse but a reflection of many human women of the time who were also left behind to mourn and wonder after their husbands sailing away.

There has been much speculation that Oðr may have in fact been Odin, although there is as much for as against this theory. The names Oðr and Odin seem to share a common linguistic root, both were said to wander or travel for extended periods, and it has been suggested that Freya herself may have been identical to Frigga (discussed further below) who was known to be married to Odin (Simek, 2007). However, mythology portrays Freya and Odin's relationship as complex and sometimes antagonistic, the two are never said or implied to be married to each other under those names, and Hnoss is never listed or described anywhere as a child of Odin which seems like an odd omission if he were in fact understood to be Oðr as well. In the end we are left with little information about Oðr, beyond his connection to Freya.

Freya is known to have a daughter, Hnoss, by her husband Oðr; Hnoss means treasure and the Prose Edda claims all things of value are called by her name because of her. Snorri also references another daughter of Freya named Gersimi, meaning jewel, but Simek suggests this may be Snorri's own invention or a confusion for Hnoss given the names are effectively synonyms (Simek, 2007). Nothing else is known about either of these figures.

Freya and Odin have a complex relationship that can be viewed as both positive and contentious. It was Freya who is said to have taught Odin seidhr and perhaps magic more generally, and some scholars argue that Odin was actually Oðr and so Freya's husband (as discussed above). However, Odin also acts against Freya in some cases, including having her famous necklace stolen so that he could force her to enchant two kings to eternally battle. Several scholars including Turville-Petre assume that Freya was, at the least, Odin's lover if not his wife and the Sörla þáttr describes her as one of Odin's many different mistresses. In a historic context it's likely that the original worship of the Vanic deities, who were focused on fertility and the dead, came into conflict with the worship of Odin and the stories about the war between the two groups as well as the tension seen between Freya and Odin may reflect the clashing of their followers (Ellis Davidson, 1964).

Freya had an often ambiguous relationship with Loki, who in one story nearly causes her to be lost to the giants and in another steals her famous necklace, Brisingamen (admittedly at Odin's behest). When Thor's hammer is stolen, however, she does lend him her falcon cloak to help recover Mjolnir and similarly, when Idunna is kidnapped by a giant, Freya lends Loki the same cloak to go and search for her.

Besides her relationships with Freyr, Oðr, and Odin, Freya was also said to have many lovers among both the gods and elves, and at least one human. Her devotee, Ottar, appears in the poem Hyndluljoð in the Poetic Edda where the giantess, Hyndla, claims he is Freya's lover, a fact that Freya doesn't outright deny and which she later seems to confirm with her actions in protecting him from the giant's ill will.

Freya By Any Other Names?

In Norse it's common for many deities, powers, and even items to have alternate poetic names called heiti or by-names. Freya, possibly because of her widespread popularity, has many such by-names each of which tells us something about this powerful goddess. Exploring her other names can help us learn more about who she is and so we're going to take a look at the main ones found across the mythology.

Gefn – a name attributed to Freya in the Prose Edda which means 'giver'. A related form of this name, Gefjon, is used for a distinct goddess which does create some confusion.

Horn – referenced in the Gylfaginning as a name of Freya, Horn is somewhat obscure. The etymology is uncertain but several scholars have suggested it may relate to 'flax'. Simek suggests that Freya could have been viewed as a goddess who protected all aspects of flax production and points out evidence in Sweden of a probable cult to Horn in this context (Simek, 2007).

Göndul – the name used by Freya in Sörla þattr when she goes in disguise to stir up strife between two kings after Odin has had Loki steal Brisingamen. The name is connected to the Old Norse word for a magic wand and is also the name of a Valkyrie (Simek, 2007).

Mardoll – found in multiple sources as a name for Freya and also used as a poetic term for gold. The meaning of the name is uncertain but is likely connected to the sea in some way; possibly it may be read as 'sea-light' (Turville-Petre, 1964).

Skjalf – given as a name for Freya in the Þulur, the only occurrence of the character as such is in the Ynglinga Saga where Skjalf appears as a human who marries a king and subsequently strangles him with her necklace. Simek suggests the necklace appearing in the story may represent a tie to Freya but the evidence is weak; Ellis Davidson suggests ties to a Vanic cult and ritual sacrifice of a king.

Syr – sow, a name connected to Freya and it should be noted in line with wider connections between Vanic deities and pigs. Both Freya and Freyr have associations with sows and boars, possibly symbolizing fertility and strength.

Valfreya – found in Njal's Saga this name means 'Lady of the Slain' and connects Freya to the dead, specifically the battle dead.

Vanadis – literally 'woman of the Vanir' a name used for Freya in the Prose Edda which reiterates her connection to the Vanir. It has also been suggested that this name may connect Freya to the dísir more generally, although that is unclear just from the term.

It should be noted that many of the names used for Freya are also used as terms for women: Freya means lady, Horn and Gefn are used as poetic terms for woman, and Heidhr was used for a witch. This may all indicate Freya's wider importance and connection to the domestic sphere associated with women of the time period.

Epithets

The Prose Edda's Skáldskaparmal describes Freya using a variety of additional by-names which also work as epithets including Daughter of Njördr, Sister of Freyr, Wife of Ódr, Mother of Hnoss, Possessor of the Slain, Possessor of Sessrúmnir, Possessor of the Gib-Cats, Possessor of Brísingamen, Goddess of the Vanir, Lady of the Vanir, Goddess Beautiful in Tears, Goddess of Love. All of these represent relationships, possessions, or attributes that are significant to Freya and help further define who she is. They also represent a common approach in Norse texts and poetry where a person or item isn't referred to directly but by referencing things connected to it that would be well known. Hence gold is called Freya's Tears or Tears of Oðr's Bed-mate because of the well-known idea that Freya cried gold while mourning her husband.

Controversial Possibilities

Besides Freya's known by-names there are also some other names that are associated with her but whose connections are more controversial. Opinions vary as to whether these names belong to distinct beings or may be Freya under a different guise, and the debate around this will likely never end. We will discuss the various possibilities and evidence supporting or contradicting them here but the reader should be aware that this is largely speculation, although some of it is more well supported than others.

Frigga – One of the most pervasive debates in both academia and modern Heathenry is about the possible connection, or lack thereof, between Freya and Frigga. I would rather not forward my own opinion here so instead I am going to offer both points of view and allow the reader to decide which they find the most persuasive.

Freya and Frigga are the same being: there is a thread of discussion in academia and in Heathenry that suggests that Freya and Frigga are in fact a singular deity known under two different names. This is supported, at least tenuously, by both being connected to Odin and possibly, if we believe that Od is in fact Odin, both married to him and by the similarity in their names, both of which ultimately mean 'woman'. In Germanic sources Frigga is known as Frija.

Freya and Frigga are unique beings: In contrast to the above possibility it is also perhaps equally likely that the two deities are unique. Their mythology is distinctive and historically they are found in different geographical areas. As well in later Norse sources where they are found together, they have different purviews which in several instances contrast with each other, for example Freya as a goddess of love and Frigga as a goddess of marriage. The two may also represent a pair within a possible trio of goddesses found across Indo-European belief, in which Freya would represent the lover and Frigga the wife as archetypes for women to call on (Ellis Davidson, 1964). In that sense Freya and Frigga are not reflections of each other but act in a complimentary way, encompassing every aspect of a woman's life in the pre-Christian period.

To summarize with a quote:

Frigga is usually considered the goddess of married love; Freya, the goddess of love, the northern Venus. Actually, Frigga is of the Aesir family of Scandinavian myth; Freya, of the Vanir family; the two lines of belief merged, and the two goddesses are sometimes fused, and sometimes confused. (Shipley, 1984)

Gullveig – Her name literally means 'gold-might', she is a controversial and obscure figure who appears only in a few stanzas of the Voluspa; it was Gullveig's death by burning at the hands of the Aesir which started the war between the Aesir and Vanir:

The war I remember, the first in the world,
When the gods with spears had smitten Gollveig,
And in the hall of Hor had burned her,
Three times burned, and three times born,
Oft and again, yet ever she lives. (Bellows, 1936)

It seems reasonably certain that Gullveig was one of the Vanir and possibly the first to interact with the Aesir, who as stated above, burned her three times after impaling her. O'Donoghue suggests that this represented a mythic retelling of the real world situation in which a woman of rank would be kidnapped or forced to marry into another group or family, suggesting that in this case Freya was known initially as Gullveig and was taken by force by the Aesir initiating the first war. This may perhaps be supported by the fact that the Eddas tell us that Njorð and Freyr were sent as peace hostages and do not mention Freya, although she appears in a pivotal role in a story very early after the end of the war.[6] Bellows compares Gullveig's burning to the process for refining gold, making the entire passage symbolic and goes on to compare Heidhr (discussed next) to the finished product of such a process. He also cites another scholar in suggesting that Gullveig is simply another name for Freya which would in turn make Gullveig and Heidhr both alternate names for Freya. This idea is considered somewhat controversial but is largely accepted by scholars.

Heidhr – Another obscure figure although she appears in several sources, referenced as a seeress. Her name means fame or light (Simek, 2007). Heidhr is also a term used across various sagas for seeresses and witches, which Simek suggests may have been used to indicate witches that were more helpful or positive. In this sense then just as Freya is a title meaning lady, Heidhr is simply another title meaning, effectively, witch. The strongest account we have of Heidhr in connection to Freya is the passage in the Voluspa which follows the burning of Gullveig:

> *Heith they named her who sought their home,*
> *The wide-seeing witch, in magic wise;*
> *Minds she bewitched that were moved by her magic,*
> *To evil women a joy she was* (Bellows, 1936)

Modern Heathens have no consensus on Heidhr although it has been suggested that the triple burning of Gullveig and magical work of Heidhr represent an initiatory experience and subsequent skillset (Blain, 2002).

Freya In My Life

I was introduced to Freya around 1999 or so by my friend Patricia Lafayllve. This was several years before my own interest in Heathenry developed but at the time, we shared other common interests and through that, and her, I came to learn of Freya. My initial understanding of the goddess was, of course, rudimentary and also shaped by my wider practices at the time which focused on witchcraft and Irish paganism so I won't say that I had the most accurate picture of who Freya was to start. But through my friend I came to see Freya as more than just 'the Lady' of the Norse pantheon and came to appreciate how complex and multi-layered Freya truly was.

As my own journey into Heathenry began several years later, I focused more on Odin but Freya and Freyr always held a special place for me: Freyr for his connection to the Ljósálfar and Freya for the strength and power that I saw within her stories.

Chapter 2

Freya in Mythology and Folklore

One important way to understand who Freya is comes from looking at her role in the mythology and later folklore. Freya's popularity is evident in the number of stories in which she appears and the usually pivotal, if passive, role she takes. People will sometimes joke that Heathenry is the 'religion with homework' because of the importance placed on the source material, especially the Eddas, but these texts really are great ways to begin to understand the various deities and to gain a feeling of who they were and are. This is as true of Freya as it is of any other deity and, by reading her stories, we can see both how she acts within the lore and also how important she is within the wider material.

This section will offer some highlights of Freya's appearances in mythology and folklore. These should be understood as recaps of the stories not retellings but are organized so that a person could seek out the original tale if they wanted to. I recommend Kevin Crossley-Holland's book *The Norse Myths* for some good retellings that put the stories together and in easy to read language.

Poetic Edda – Written by an unknown author or authors in the 13th century the Poetic Edda, as it is known today, contains a selection of important works discussing pre-Christian beliefs. The main manuscript the material is drawn from is the Codex Regius which contains 31 poems. A selection of these will be discussed here which specifically mention Freya.

The Voluspa relates the creation of the world and prophecies its eventual destruction. In the poem the seeress describes the first war of the Aesir, wherein they burned the Vanic woman

Gullveig (who may, as previously discussed, be Freya). This act started a war between the two groups which the Vanir eventually won and after which peace hostages were exchanged, including Njorð, Freyr and Freya. The poem also gives a brief account of Freya as Oðr's wife and recounts a tale, told in full in the Prose Edda, where a giant asks for Freya as his prize for building a wall around Asgard.

In the Grimnismal we are told that Freya's hall is called Sessrumnir, 'rich in seats', and is located on Fólkvangr, 'field of folk', where it is listed 9th among a list of the homes of the various Aesir. We are also told that Freya is given her choice among the battle dead every day, claiming half of them, while Odin gets the other half.

In the Lokasenna, a flyting[7] story, Loki insults everyone who has gathered for a party in Aegir's hall in a stylized format where he insults one person, another defends them, and he moves on to insulting that person and so on. Freya appears in the story after Loki has insulted Frigga, cautioning him that it is foolish to insult her as she knows the fates of all beings. Loki turns to insulting Freya by accusing her of having had sex with all the Gods and elves in the hall; she in turn replies that he is lying to stir up trouble because he knows the gods are furious with him. He responds to that by claiming that she was caught by the Aesir mid-coitus with her brother Freyr at which point Freya farted. Then Njorð intervenes to defend her by claiming there is no harm in a woman having a husband and lovers and the text moves on.

The Þrymskviða is perhaps one of the most comedic of the Poetic Edda tales and describes the events that occur when Mjolnir is stolen by one of the giants. When Thor realizes Mjolnir is gone, he goes to Loki, and the two in turn go to Freya to see if she will lend her falcon cloak so that Loki can travel across the realms in search of the hammer. She agrees, because of the immense value of Mjolnir in protecting the Gods, and

Loki uses it to transform into a falcon. He returns later and says that the giant, Þrym, has hidden the hammer and will return it only if Freya is given to him as his wife, an announcement that is met with great rage from the goddess. Asgard shakes with her anger, she roars, Brisingamen falls from her neck, and she declares that she would have to be the most lustful of beings to agree to go to the giants (in other words, she absolutely will not do it). As an alternative the god Heimdallr suggests that Thor should go in her place disguised as a bride with a veil over his face. This plan is adopted and Thor goes in this disguise with Loki by his side dressed as a handmaiden. All would be lost early on to Thor's temper if not for Loki's cleverness: when 'Freya' eats and drinks a huge amount Loki claims it is because she has been so eager for the wedding she has been fasting and when 'Freya' frightens Þrym with 'her' glaring eyes Loki explains that she simply hasn't slept from excitement. When the hammer is finally brought forth to bless the bride Thor throws off the disguise and attacks Þrym and the giants in his hall.

One of the most significant stories featuring Freya is also in the Poetic Edda, in the Hyndluljóð, with a description of an encounter between her and a giantess. Freya is compelled by a human named Ottar to go to the giantess to seek information about Ottar's lineage, because he has prayed to her so fervently that her altar shines like glass from the offerings, although it is elsewhere stated that Ottar was her lover as well so that may also be a motivating factor. To accomplish this Freya turns Ottar into the boar Hildisvíni and rides him to Jotunheim to find Hyndla. Once there Freya and Hyndla engage in a long conversation as Freya rides the boar and Hyndla rides a wolf to go to Valhalla to speak to Odin. Hyndla is called a volva or seeress and Freya refers to her as 'sister' implying that both fill this role. Although Hyndla sees through Freya's deception about her boar, which she claims is borrowed from her brother, the giantess nonetheless relates all of Ottar's relatives back to establish the lineage claim he is looking for. At the end of Hyndla's recitation Freya request that 'her boar' be given a drink to preserve his memory of what was said at which point the exchange turns threatening; Hyndla refuses and insults Freya (by calling her a she-goat who takes many lovers besides her husband) who in turn threatens to surround the giantess in a circle of fire to hold her until she agrees. Hyndla then promises a drink that will curse Ottar instead, to which Freya replies that she will see him blessed by the gods and kept safe from Hyndla's harm.

Prose Edda – Written in the 13th century by Icelandic scholar Snorri Sturluson, the material often references other now lost manuscripts or stories providing hints of earlier beliefs. The Prose Edda is seen as an important document that gives us a glimpse into pre-Christian beliefs although it was composed during the Christian period in Iceland. It consists of four main sections, but we will only be looking at the two here that concern Freya.

Gylfaginning is the second section of the Prose Edda, following the prologue, and depicts a conversation between a human and Odin in disguise after the human enters Asgard seeking answers. Through a series of question and answer style prose Odin relates the creation of the world and describes the Aesir and their homes in Asgard. When he reaches the Vanir, he says this:

Njördr in Nóatún begot afterward two children: the son was called Freyr, and the daughter Freyja; they were fair of face and mighty…. Freyja is the most renowned of the goddesses; she has in heaven the dwelling called Fólkvangr, and wheresoever she rides to the strife, she has one-half of the kill, and Odin half, as is here said:

Fólkvangr 't is called, where Freyja rules
    Degrees of seats in the hall;

Half the kill she keepeth each day,
  And half Odin hath.

Her hall Sessrúmnir is great and fair. When she goes forth, she drives her cats and sits in a chariot; she is most conformable to man's prayers, and from her name comes the name of honor, Frú, by which noblewomen are called. Songs of love are well-pleasing to her; it is good to call on her for furtherance in love. (Brodeur, 1916).

In a later passage where all the goddesses of the Aesir are being discussed, Freya is referred to as 'most gently born' and it is said that she was married to Oðr and had a daughter Hnoss by him. He would travel and disappear for periods during which she would cry tears of 'red gold' and assume various disguise names to search for him. Finally, the text relates that she possesses the necklace Brisingamen and is called 'Lady of the Vanir'.

In the section explaining how Odin's steed Sleipnir came to be born we learn that a giant had come to the Gods offering to build a great wall around Asgard for protection but he demanded Freya, the sun, and the moon as payment. Loki convinced the Aesir to agree and to set a timeline for completion that seemed impossible, but when the giant was on track to finish on time the Aesir compelled Loki to intercede because they were afraid of losing Freya to the giants. Loki, knowing that the giant was working so quickly because he was aided by a stallion, took the form of a mare and lured him away so that the work could not be completed. Later Loki gave birth to the eight legged horse Sleipnir.

The final reference here to Freya is a simple note that she drove her cat-pulled chariot to attend Baldur's funeral.

Skáldskaparmal is the third section in the Prose Edda and begins by describing a feast held in Aegir's hall which the Aesir are attending; Freya is listed second (after Frigga) among the

Asynjur[8] who are guests. Following passages in this portion do not directly mention Freya but reference her when discussing Njorð as father of Freyr and Freya, Freyr as Freya's brother, and Heimdallr as the one who recovered Freya's stolen necklace.

A later passage describes the giant Hrungnir chasing Odin to Asgard and then drinking in the Aesir's hall. Growing drunk the giant boasts that he will destroy Asgard and take Freya and Sif[9] back with him; only Freya is brave enough to continue serving him mead after this point. When the giant's threats become too much, Thor is called and bursts into the hall, angry that Hrungnir has been allowed there and that Freya is serving him *as if at a feast of the Aesir* (Brodeur, 1916).

In the 20th Chapter of the section we get a detailed list of Freya's epithets:

> *How should one periphrase Freyja? Thus: by calling her Daughter of Njördr, Sister of Freyr, Wife of Ódr, Mother of Hnoss, Possessor of the Slain, of Sessrúmnir, of the Gib-Cats, and of Brísinga-men; Goddess of the Vanir, Lady of the Vanir, Goddess Beautiful in Tears, Goddess of Love. All the goddesses may be periphrased thus: by calling them by the name of another, and naming them in terms of their possessions or their works or their kindred.* (Brodeur, 1916)

A later passage explains that Freya's Tears is used as a kenning or poetic expression for gold, referring to her here by several of the names mentioned above: Mardoll, Mother of Hnoss, Wife of Oðr, Daughter of Njorð, Sister of Freyr, Gefn, and Bride of the Vanir in a short poetic verse about gold. The author concludes by saying that any of these terms along with 'tears' are acceptable poetic names for gold, referring back to the belief that Freya cried tears of gold for Oðr:

> *It is proper to join 'tears' with all the names of Freyja, and to call gold by such terms; and in divers ways these periphrases have been*

varied, so that gold is called Hail, or Rain, or Snow-Storm, or Drops, or Showers, or Water falls, of Freyja's Eyes, or Cheeks, or Brows, or Eyelids. (Brodeur, 1916).

Heimskringla – Another 13th century work by Snorri Sturluson the Heimskringla is a collection of shorter texts relating tales of various kings. Freya appears in a euhemerized form in the first of these texts, the Ynglinga Saga although much of her divine presence is retained even in this guise. She is described, as in other works, as the daughter of Njorð and his unnamed sister and sister to Freyr, as a member of the Vanir, and as a peace hostage to the Aesir after the end of the war between the Vanir and Aesir. Odin appoints Freya the priestess over sacrificial offerings and she in turn teaches seidhr to the Aesir, as it was a Vanic skill.

Eventually in the tale Freya was the last survivors of either the Vanir or Aesir and Freya becomes famous for her role as a priestess. So great does her fame grow that the text claims this is why Freya's name was used as a title for ladies and explains the source of the term 'husfreya' – lady of the house – as deriving from Freya's name to describe women who owned land.

Her husband Oðr is also mentioned as is her daughter Hnoss as well as a second daughter Gersimi (possible a duplicate of Hnoss); Freya is described as very clever and her daughters as the most beautiful in the world.

Egil's Saga – A 13th century Icelandic saga. Freya is mentioned in a reference in this text, when the main character's daughter states that she will not eat (as her father is also on a hunger fast) until she dies and goes to Freya's hall.

Hálfs saga ok Hálfsrekka – Freya is mentioned in passing in this story, as a goddess whom a woman calls on to help her brew mead. The woman's rival calls on Odin for the same purpose and ultimately wins the competition the two women are in, not because Freya failed to answer but because Odin made a deal with the second woman to give him something he wanted in exchange for victory.

Sörla þáttr – A 14th century text which features some stories about Freya. It begins by saying Freya was the daughter of Njorð and one of Odin's mistresses, then describes Freya's encounter with four dwarves who were master craftsmen. Seeing a magnificent necklace that the dwarves had created Freya attempts to buy it but is rebuffed – the dwarves say they will only give it to her if she spends a night with each of them in turn. Desperate to gain the beautiful necklace Freya agrees and four days later emerges with the necklace.

Loki finds out that she has it and tells Odin who orders him to steal it. Loki then sneaks into Freya's room disguised as a fly and finds her sleeping with the necklace still on. He changes into the shape of a flea and bites her so that she will roll over and he will be able to unclasp the necklace. He leaves her still soundly sleeping and takes the necklace back to Odin; when Freya confronts Odin about the theft, he says he will only return the necklace to her if she agrees to use her magic to enspell two kings and 20 lords so that they will eternally fight, rising each day from the dead to continue their battle, until freed by a Christian king.[10] Freya reluctantly agrees and gains her necklace back. The story then moves on to describe tales of the mortal protagonists.

Although never named in the tale it is widely assumed that the necklace in question is Brisingamen and this story is given in retellings and modern accounts as the story of how Freya acquired it.

Folklore – Unsurprisingly Freya survived in folklore across the last centuries, both in material based on the older Eddas and Sagas and in newer folk beliefs. One 19th century Swedish account describes Freya as the source of harmless cloud to cloud lightning, particularly in connection to the Rye harvest, and it was also said that Freya would visit apple orchards in the winter to encourage a good harvest (Schön, 2004).

There have also been several Victorian era retellings of Freya's stories which have, unsurprisingly, altered the stories enough to make them unique versions, as well as other more modern books in the same vein. I'll briefly describe two here that have had an impact on current belief for some people.

Padraic Colum's 1920 *The Children of Odin* features a retelling of how Freya gained her necklace that combines it with the loss of Oðr to create a blatant morality tale. In this version Freya decides to go to Earth to seek out three banished giants. Although she is queen of the elves, they will not help her find her way and eventually she runs across a group of dwarves who agree to show her if she promises to stay one night with them. She agrees and they proceed to force their affection on her and beat her when she tries to resist. The next day they show her to the giants who give her Brisingamen but she already regrets seeking them out. When she returns to her home, she finds that her husband, 'Odur' has fled because of what she did to get the necklace and she learns that he will never return to her. The story ends with her wearing Brisingamen not as a point of power or pride but as a mark of shame, a reminder of her actions.

In the 1923 work *The Stories of the Months and Days* by Reginald Couzens we find an account of Freya that includes several features which have worked their way into wider belief today. She is described as blue eyed and blond, wearing a cloak of feathers, and was called the goddess of love and beauty. Couzens relates a story of Freya and her husband, Odur, saying that Odur left once and Freya went seeking after him weeping so that the tears that fell on land were gold and those that fell in the sea were amber. All of nature mourned with her and autumn and then winter came in response to her grief, until finally Freya found Odur 'in the sunny south' and all of nature rejoiced at their reunion, causing spring to come to the land. The author goes on to give a retelling of the loss of Thor's hammer except that instead of lending her falcon cloak, Freya lends Brisingamen to Thor to aid his disguise, which causes Loki to covet it and eventually steal it.

This is only a brief recap of Freya's wider place in mythology and folklore but hopefully it has shown the importance she had in the stories and the way these myths have grown and changed over time. I strongly suggest people interested in Freya read the original versions for themselves if possible. Many can be found free online.

Freya In My Life

My personal favourite myth of Freya is her acquisition of Brisingamen. Although this can be one of her more controversial stories it has always struck me as a very powerful tale – not of morality or lust, as some people interpret it – but of a deity claiming their main symbol for themselves through their own agency. When we look at how the other Norse gods gained their treasures, including Mjolnir and Draupnir, they were created by the dwarves through Loki's trickery in a wider bid for Loki to appease the Aesir after offending Thor's wife Sif. They were, in effect, peace gifts. But not Freya's necklace; Brisingamen was something that Freya went out and gained for herself in a way that reminds me of Odin gaining the runes through self-sacrifice.

It was not passively gifted to her or given as recompense for an offense but is a prize she set her sights on and earned for herself. For me this is a vital part of what I see Brisingamen symbolizing: sexuality and personal power. Freya is in control of these aspects of herself. While I do appreciate the way that the overt sexuality in the story makes some people uncomfortable or has made others go to great lengths to try to sanitize or explain away for me that part of the story is powerful and important.

Chapter 3

Associations, Animals, and Possessions

Freya is a complicated deity with various associations and connections throughout the myths and folklore, many of which have been touched on in the first two chapters. Here I'd like to dive a bit deeper into these associations and explore what we may be able to learn about her by looking at what is so often connected to her. Just as reading her stories can help us get to know her better, we can also get closer to understanding who and what Freya is by looking at the animals, items, and things that are connected to her. These give us clues to her personality and also as polytheists give us ways to relate to her as a deity.

Love – Freya is often described as a goddess of love and 19th and 20th century sources often compared her to Venus. In the Grimnismal we are told that Freya enjoys love songs and that she is a good choice to pray to in matters of love; she is strongly connected with the wider concepts of both love and sex. It should be noted that the love poetry which Freya favoured was prohibited or limited in Icelandic law[11] (Turville-Petre, 1964). In the Lokasenna, Loki accuses her of having all of the Aesir and elves for lovers, while in the Hyndluloð the giantess, Hyndla, compares her to a she-goat and says that though her husband, Oðr, loved her dearly she still took many other lovers as well. While this may not establish her as a 'Venus' figure per se it does imply that she would have a sympathy for humans in similar situations and that she had an interest in matters of love, married or otherwise. Ellis Davidson also suggests that her connections to oracular seidhr which included human practitioners predicting marriages would tie Freya into the wider concepts of love and marriage and may reflect aspects of the older Vanic worship.

And it may be worth noting that just as freya was used as a word for women, her name was also a poetic term or term of endearment used in several texts by men speaking of their beloved (Lindow, 2001).

Sex[12] – Freya is not a goddess of sex, per se, but sex is one of her associations due to her portrayal throughout the lore. She is married but known to take lovers, including the human, Ottar. She earns Brisingamen through sex with the dwarves who made it and she is coveted as a prize among the giants (O'Donoghue, 2008). She is a being who is comparatively open sexually and in control of her own sexuality, something that would have been notable even in the pre-Christian era. The Icelanders in particular were a law-driven people who had punishments for many of the sexual activities that we see Freya engaging in, and yet her popularity as a deity remained even after conversion. It is possible that this is because Freya's stories, and those of the Aesir more generally, may have reflected the actual sexual mores and activities of people more accurately than the strict law texts reflected (Guðmundsson, 2016). It is also possible that Freya represented a sexual ideal that transcended people's daily lives.

Most scholars tie sex and fertility intrinsically together so that Freya as a fertility goddess cannot ultimately be separated from Freya as a sexual being. Ellis Davidson argues (relying on Eliade) that sex, including sexual activity like orgies which would be outside acceptable behaviour, were inherent parts of fertility cults and would have played a role in Vanic worship. Post-Christian commentators and some modern scholars like Turville-Petre go to lengths to criticize Freya's open sexuality and sexual practices, overlaying strong Christian morality onto the pre-Christian goddess so that she becomes a goddess whose choices are based on lust rather than genuine desire or a greater good. I would suggest that readers of Freya's stories make an effort to look past these judgements and see the stories as they are in their own context, and to ask themselves why a goddess so often reviled for her 'promiscuity' is also said – by Snorri Sturluson – to have been the longest lasting of the Aesir and to have remained popular into the modern period. By the laws of the time and by modern standards Freya can be argued to be promiscuous yet when we dig past those external judgements what we find is, perhaps, a deity whose sexuality and sexual activity is part of her wider powers of fertility and wealth (Lafayllve, 2006). What we end up with then is a goddess who acts outside common sexual mores both as an expression of her own agency and to correctly direct the gifts which she gives; refusing to go with unworthy suitors, such as Þrym but choosing those who deserve her attention.

Fertility – As a Vanic goddess Freya's association with fertility is assumed (Simek, 2007; Lindow, 2001). The Vanir more generally are viewed as fertility gods and seen to take on rolls associated with fertility, both in blessing the earth and around human procreation. One story in the Poetic Edda relates a prayer after a successful birth which calls on, among others, Freya and it has been suggested that her necklace may be representative of historic birthing charms (Blain, 2002).

Lindow points to the linking of Frey and Freya across the stories as an indication that they may have fulfilled the Dumézilian third function role as fertility deities because gods in this function are often paired or twins. This may also relate to the overt sexuality of both and their relationship to each other. While this may seem distasteful or even contradictory to modern practitioners it has been suggested that historic fertility cults would have included an emphasis on ecstasy and unbridled sex which would have been more accepting of such blatant moral boundary crossing (Ellis Davidson, 1964).

The link between Freya and fertility is further shored up by her wider connections to both love and the dead, purviews that often coincide with fertility gods (Lindow, 2001). Further to this, Turville-Petre also suggests that the reason the giants often request Freya and that the giant building Asgard's walls asked for Freya and the sun and moon, is that she represents fertility and successful procreation; by taking her the giants would plunge the world into barrenness and by taking her and the sun and moon would create an endless winter.[13]

Seidhr – We will tackle Freya's connection to magic in more depth in the next chapter but it needs to be noted here that she was a deity of such, most particularly of the practice of seidhr. In the modern day many people consider her more widely a deity of magic in general and of witches.

The Dead – Freya is not directly connected to the dead in her stories but we may suggest a less direct connection via the Vanir and seidhr. Some seidhr practices involved calling on contacting the dead, especially to gain information, and working with the dead would be understood as within the realm of seidhrwork. The Vanir represented gods of fertility and the earth and there is an intrinsic tie between those things and the dead (Ellis Davidson, 1964). This may be more clearly demonstrated by looking at Freyr's stories than Freya's but the wider concepts can be argued.

Battle Dead – Freya is connected to those who die in battle, of whom she gets her choice over Odin; the implication being that Freya chooses first and Odin gets the remaining half. It is important to note here that Freya's connection is specifically to those who die in battle, not the dead more generally, which is one of several points of direct intersection with Odin's purviews. While we know that Odin is gathering slain warriors to fight at

Ragnarök it is unclear why Freya claims half the battle dead or what she does with them and we are not told her fate in Ragnarök.

Freya's exact connection to the dead and battle dead is obscure. It has been suggested by Ellis Davidson that it ties into her role as a fertility goddess, with life and death intrinsically linked. Turville-Petre goes the furthest in suggesting Freya as a goddess of war and death due to her association with the battle dead, and one might assume her stirring up of war at Odin's request, but most other scholars are less comfortable with those labels for her.

Valkyries – Although not explicitly stated it is implied in several sources that Freya may either act as a Valkyrie or leads the Valkyries. The Grimnismal reference to her getting a choice among the battle dead may support this as does a reference in Njal's Saga to Freya as 'Valfreya' or Freya of the Slain. Additionally in the Sörla þattr when Odin forces Freya to start an endless war between two kings she does so in disguise using the name Göndul, which is elsewhere given in various lists of Valkyrie names; while this is far from conclusive it may be considered evidence supporting Freya's association with the Valkyries more generally.

Dísir – The Dísir are female ancestral spirits thought to guard over their descendants, although they appear in a much grimmer form in the lore. The references to dísir that can be found across different textual sources usually appear before someone is about to die and often reference the dísir being angry or dangerous, suggesting that they have withdrawn their protection from a warrior and are there to seal his fate (Lindow, 2011). They may be related to the Valkyries; however, modern heathens tend to look to them as positive protective figures. Freya is called Vanadis which may be read as woman of the Vanir or possibly as Vanic Dísir which has led some people to connect her to these spirits in a similar way to Freyr being associated with the Alfar. Interpretations are, as usual, complicated by the meaning of dís, which is simply 'woman'.

Falcon cloak – Mentioned in the Þrymskviða and Skáldskaparmal, Freya's falcon cloak is an item which allows the person wearing it to shape shift into the form of a falcon. It is only seen in these two stories being used by Loki after he has gained the loan of it from Freya but the implication is that the cloak is one of her special possessions and something that she is able to use, perhaps in line with her practice of Seidhr and shapeshifting.

Brisingamen – Of uncertain etymology, Brisingamen is often given as 'necklace of the Brisings'.[14] However, Simek suggests that it may more likely be understood as 'shining necklace' which does better suit it in context. The exact nature of Brisingamen is somewhat ambiguous and although most sources refer to it as a necklace it has also been given in translation as everything from a collar to torque to girdle. The only thing agreed on across the sources is that it was a woman's jewellery ornament most likely worn around the neck. Based on the way it was created by four dwarves it is possible the necklace itself had a four part construction or layering, but this can only be speculated on (Gundarsson, 2006).

One of the most famous stories about Freya hinges on her acquiring the necklace Brisingamen, although it is not given that name in the story, from four dwarves who created it, and this story can be found in the older mythic material as well across modern retellings. The story is often read with moral overtones, however, despite the range of interpretations the necklace is her primary treasure and strongly associated with her. Descriptions of the necklace itself – also called a belt and a cuff – are limited so artistic depictions vary widely. Some people envision it as a necklace of gold while others see it as amber or gold with various jewels.

Scholars have debated for decades over the possible symbolism of Brisingamen, and modern Heathens still have various ways of understanding the necklace. Simek outlines several of the main theories in his *Dictionary of Northern Mythology* including:

- Represents the aurora borealis and by extension the dead who fall in battle.
- Symbolizes the rising sun.
- Represents fertility.
- Is connected to a real world charm worn by women during childbirth.
- The theft of Brisingamen by Loki represents the theft of primordial fire.

Brisingamen features in several fragmentary stories not directly connected to Freya as well, in which the necklace has been stolen by Loki and the God Heimdallr fights to recover it. In some versions, such as the one found in Skáldskaparmál, the two gods fight in the form of seals and this same text gives Heimdallr the epithet 'bringer of Freya's necklace' (Simek, 2007).

Cats – Freya is said to travel in a chariot pulled by two cats, probably wild cats. The Grimnismal doesn't tell us or even hint at what kind of cats they may be, saying only *"Whenever Freya travels, she sits in her carriage which is drawn by cats"*. The Skáldskaparmal refers to them as 'gib-cats' an antiquated term for male cats, possible neutered. The actual term used in the original language for the animals is vague and they have been depicted in art as everything from small house cats to wild cats, although in modern folklore and belief they are usually envisioned as large cats.

Her ownership of these cats[15] has been the source of much speculation among scholars. O'Donoghue suggest they may represent chaos as a chariot pulled by cats would seem to be a difficult option. Turville-Petre sees the cats as representing lust, saying: *"The cat, as the Norse pagans must have known, is the most lascivious of beasts."* (Turville-Petre, 1964). Ellis Davidson takes the most benevolent view and ascribes the cat association to Freya's connection to seidhr and the cat's reputation as a supernatural animal.

In the older sources these animals are never named, however, Diana Paxson in her 1984 novel, *Brisingamen*, chose to name the cats Bygull (Beegold) and Tregull (Treegold) as modern poetic kennings of Honey and Amber.[16] These names have gained popularity across modern pagan books and can be found in several such texts given as if they are the original mythic names of the cats.

While it is generally assumed today, and has been across artwork for many years, that the cats are indeed cats there is some question around the original word used. Older translators have no hesitation to give the word as cats or tom-cats, but Grimm in *Teutonic Mythology* questioned whether bear wasn't the intended term and an assortment of other animals, including weasels, have also been suggested. Despite this there is reasonable evidence that some form of either wild or domestic cat was meant and would have been understood by the contemporary audience (Gundarsson, 2006).

Hildisvíni – Literally battle boar although Freya claims he is Gullinbursti, 'gold bristled' a magical boar created by the dwarves which belongs to Freyr. Freya says she is riding this boar in the Hyndluð and while she isn't – it's actually her devoted lover, Ottar, shape changed – it may be read by implication that Freya also made use of the magical boar when she needed to, or could borrow it from her brother. In either case both Freyr and Freya are associated with boar riding.

Pigs – In a more general sense pigs are associated with both Freyr and Freya. One of Freya's names is Syr, meaning sow, she turns her lover, Ottar, into a boar, and may be able to take such a shape herself as well (Turville-Petre, 1964). It has also been suggested that the yule boar would be sacred to both Freya and Freyr (Gundarsson, 2006). Pigs are animals that can represent fertility, warriors, death, and abundance – all things that relate to Freya personally and the Vanir more generally.

Falcon – Because she possesses the falcon cloak and can take the shape of a falcon, the bird is more generally associated with her.

Gold – In the Eddas we are told that Freya cried tears of gold over her lost husband Oðr. This metal is strongly associated with Freya, so much so that there are a dozen poetic names for gold that reference Freya one way or another, and her daughters Hnoss and Gersimi may serve as figurative references to golden treasure. If we assume that Gullveig and Heidhr are other names for Freya then we see the layers of connection deepened as both of those figures are named after or referencing gold. Turville-Petre even suggests that Freya's original appearance among the Aesir may relate to the arrival of gold lust or greed.

In a wider sense just as Freya was a goddess of fertility and abundance in the sense of propagation, she is also a goddess of abundance of a more material nature. She wept tears of literal gold and her daughters were named 'treasure', and she herself may have been a symbol of wealth and riches – yet another reason the giants wanted to gain her so badly (Lindow, 2001).

Amber – Freya has a strong modern association with amber, and while it isn't a reference in older myths you will find newer stories suggesting she cried tears of amber rather than gold. It is possible that the Brisingamen, her famous necklace, was of amber or included amber (Ellis Davidson, 1964).

Jet – Sometimes found alongside amber in amulets or spindle whorls, jet was associated with Freya and may have been known as "black amber" (Ward, 2022).

Friday – The sixth day of the week is named Friday after Freya according to some Icelandic sources who called the day Freyjudagr, literally 'Freya's Day' (Harper, 2022). This varied by location, however, as in areas of Germany without Freya's presence the day was named for Frigga. Modern Heathens continue to debate this but for those who are so inclined Friday can be seen as Freya's day and used for offerings to her.

Folkvangir – Found only in a single reference in the Grimnismal, repeated in the Prose Edda, folkvangir means 'army field' or field of the army in early old Norse (Crawford, 2022). In most modern sources and references you will see the name given 'field of the people or folk' using the later meaning of folk rather than the earlier one that existed when the Grimnismal was recorded. Folkvangir is said to be the 9th hall of the gods, belonging to Freya, listed among the other halls of the Aesir. Freya chooses half the battle dead (Odin gets the other half) and the implication[17] is that they go to her hall on Folkvangir.

Sessrumnir – Freya's hall the name means 'many seats' (Simek, 2007). While the Norse afterlife does not function as others may assume there is an implication that some humans may go to Freya's hall after death, with Freya claiming half the battle dead for herself as well as at least one reference to a non-combatant who expected to go there. In Egil's Saga, Egil's daughter,

Thorgerd, refuses to eat and says *"nor will I do so until I join Freyja"* (Scudder, 2011).

Plants – Common Milkwort, Polygala vulagris, was known in Sweden as Freya's Tears or Freya's Hair (Schön, 2004).

Stars – Although it's unclear whether this is more properly attributed to Freya or Frigga, Schön suggests that the constellation Orion was previously known as Frejerock, which may be read as Freya's Distaff.

Physical locations – Although there is no surviving evidence of a cult to Freya her importance and power is shown in the multitude of place names in Sweden and Norway dedicated to her. These names range from things like Freya's temple to Freya's house or Freya's field, and include a range of natural objects like rocks and lakes as well (Simek, 2007; Turville-Petre, 1964).

Fehu – The elder futhark rune fehu is associated with Freya today (Gundarsson, 2006). The first rune of the first aett is called Fehu, or Feoh, and it is equivalent to the letter F in English. In the Anglo-Saxon poem it is equated to having wealth and being generous. In both the Norwegian and Icelandic poems it is compared to the envy that wealth can cause among family members. Most modern practitioners find its strongest connection is to domestic cattle, keeping in mind that a thousand years ago cattle in many cases were the measure of a person's wealth, much like cash is today. In terms of wealth it is the kind that requires care and nourishment to maintain, and so also represents hard work earning rewards. Fehu is the kind of wealth that must be overseen and nurtured to thrive. Since it is connected to domestic cattle which must be cared for in order to be productive, it can be both fragile and transitory. It speaks of enjoying things while you have them, as well as good husbandry of wealth, and the reward of hard work.

When the runes are used for divination it can represent wealth, generosity, investment, finances, money, and honour through giving. On the negative side it can represent the jealousy of the lazy for the industrious, the envy of those who do not want to work for things but want them handed over, and family infighting over money and strife due to money. When used in magic it would symbolize prosperity.

Freya In My Life

For me, amber has always been a main symbol of Freya. I have a distinct memory of the first time I saw my friend's shrine for Freya, a statue that was covered in amber necklaces, and thinking how strikingly beautiful it was. When I created my own small home shrine for Freya, I set about accumulating amber for it as well; something that I was able to do thanks to another friend. I dedicated several raw amber necklaces to Freya, given as offerings, which were kept in a wooden bowl near her statue. It isn't gold, of course, but there's something more evocative about amber to me – it feels alive somehow.

Amber has been used by humans for at least 10,000 years, with amber beads and carved items appearing in archaeological finds. It was used for jewellery as well as placed with the dead in ways that could imply ritual use. And it was used continuously by humans through today, as adornment, for priestesses, as a sign of rank, and across folk belief in charms. In a way it has stayed with humanity as persistently as Freya has.

Amber has a long history in folk belief relating to protection and healing. In parts of Europe it was thought to help asthma; it was also worn by teething babies because it was believed to reduce the pain. It was worn or carried for protection from injury and death and was a stone (or more properly fossilized resin) of luck. It is also associated across several cultures with love and happiness.

We don't have any stories of Freya crying tears of amber but there is a Lithuanian story about a sea goddess who did so as she mourned her lover, and it reminds me of Freya.

Chapter 4

Freya and Seidhr

It is said that Freya is the one who taught magic, specifically seidhr, to the Aesir and possibly one that Freya herself was uniquely knowledgeable in. This is a skill that she brings to the Aesir from the Vanir and one that she is said to have taught to both Odin as well as human women,[18] at least if we agree that Heidhr is another name for Freya. Seidhr itself occupies a unique place in Norse lore, being described as both a prestigious art and also something considered dangerous, as a powerful skill of women and something that men could do but not without social cost to their reputation (Ward, 2022). In many ways seidhr can be understood much as Freya is understood – highly valuable but also controversial, especially as Christianity gained power, and I think to better understand Freya we must also better understand the magic that was so uniquely hers so here we will discuss seidhr, what it was and what it is today for many modern practitioners.

Seidhr is a Norse word with an uncertain meaning that is often translated as witchcraft, or less commonly as shamanism[19] (I favour the witchcraft translation although neither is really a good English descriptor for what seidhr work encompasses). An older theory suggested by Jakob Grimm, but which is still used, suggests that Seidhr is connected to the English term 'seethe' through magical work that involved boiling water and metaphorically through the burning or refining of Gullveig into Heidhr. The word may, however, alternately be related to the word for seat and sitting is mentioned in the practice of oracular Seidhr lending some credence to this idea (Ward, 2022).

Seidhr had something of a bad reputation in the lore and can also sometimes be looked down on today because it is connected to the manipulation of others, particularly influencing a person's mind, and Blain suggests that mental illusion or influence is the primary factor involved in seidhr. It is also sometimes regarded negatively because of its connections with the concept of ergi, a term (which like seidhr) doesn't easily translate but is connected to the idea of sexual passivity. Both men and women who practice seidhr are considered ergi in some sources, with the context towards men implying homosexuality or sexual receptiveness, while in women it denotes promiscuity, an aspect that would apply to Freya in the mythology (Blain, 2002). Ward suggests that the concept of ergi around seidhr may relate to aspects of spirit work that would involve possession by spirits or gods and would therefore go against the wider culture's ideas about manliness.

Seidhr also has a predictive aspect and there was a related practice, spá or spae, which was more oracular in nature. There was a slight technical nuance between the two in terms of oracular work, as a spae worker intuited information while a seidhr worker called spirits to herself to answer questions, although this nuance is often lost or glossed over and is mostly ignored in modern usage. Predicting the future, or more accurately reading the fates that have been laid out, is a significant aspect of seidhr work and is done both passively, as in oracular work, as well as more actively in practices that seek to influence a person's fate. Fate is often visualized or described as a weaving or thread and we find evidence that physical weaving and the tools of spinning did play a role in seidhr. The distaff, a tool for spinning, seems to have been a significant tool for influencing fate and inducing trance and may connect to further, likely Vanic, practices involving elves (Heath, 2021). Fate could be influenced in positive or negative ways by working magic directly into cloth via weaving as well. There is an account in Orkneyinga Saga of a spell being woven into cloth which then affected the wearer and several accounts across the stories of protective magic being woven into clothing; this sort of woven magic was important enough that later Christian commentators went out of their way to criticize it (Ward, 2022).

According to Ynglinga Saga seidhr workers were given specific powers: controlling the weather, stilling the ocean, turning the wind, putting out fires, shapeshifting (particularly by releasing their spirit in an animal form), predicting the future, and speaking to the dead as well as blessing others with long life or good health. On the more malefic end they could bring death, illness, or bad luck. We find these skills and abilities mentioned across various sources, for example the Voluspa mentions the seidhr worker's ability to influence the minds of other people and to use magic charms, and Eric the Red's Saga talks about spirit communication and telling the future.

The best extant account of oracular seidhr work in practice comes from Erik the Red's Saga, in Chapter 4. This translation is in the public domain so I would like to give the passage in full so the reader can get the entire context:

There was in the settlement the woman whose name was Thorbjorg. She was a prophetess (spae-queen), and was called Litilvolva (little sybil). She had had nine sisters, and they were all spae-queens, and she was the only one now living.

It was a custom of Thorbjorg, in the winter time, to make a circuit, and people invited her to their houses, especially those who had any curiosity about the season, or desired to know their fate; and inasmuch as Thorkell was chief franklin thereabouts, he considered that it concerned him to know when the scarcity which overhung the settlement should cease. He invited, therefore, the spae-queen to his house, and prepared for her a hearty welcome, as was the custom wherever a reception was accorded a woman of this kind. A high seat was prepared for her, and a cushion laid thereon in which were poultry-feathers.

Now, when she came in the evening, accompanied by the man

who had been sent to meet her, she was dressed in such wise that she had a blue mantle over her, with strings for the neck, and it was inlaid with gems quite down to the skirt. On her neck she had glass beads. On her head she had a black hood of lambskin, lined with ermine. A staff she had in her hand, with a knob thereon; it was ornamented with brass, and inlaid with gems round about the knob. Around her she wore a girdle of soft hair, and therein was a large skin-bag, in which she kept the talismans needful to her in her wisdom. She wore hairy calf-skin shoes on her feet, with long and strong-looking thongs to them, and great knobs of latten at the ends. On her hands she had gloves of ermine-skin, and they were white and hairy within.

Now, when she entered, all men thought it their bounden duty to offer her becoming greetings, and these she received according as the men were agreeable to her. The franklin Thorkell took the wise-woman by the hand, and led her to the seat prepared for her. He requested her to cast her eyes over his herd, his household, and his homestead. She remained silent altogether.

During the evening the tables were set; and now I must tell you what food was made ready for the spae-queen. There was prepared for her porridge of kid's milk, and hearts of all kinds of living creatures there found were cooked for her. She had a brazen spoon, and a knife with a handle of walrus-tusk, which was mounted with two rings of brass, and the point of it was broken off.

When the tables were removed, the franklin Thorkell advanced to Thorbjorg and asked her how she liked his homestead, or the appearance of the men; or how soon she would ascertain that which he had asked, and which the men desired to know. She replied that she would not give answer before the morning, after she had slept there for the night.

And when the (next) day was far spent, the preparations were made for her which she required for the exercise of her enchantments. She begged them to bring to her those women who were acquainted with the lore needed for the exercise of the enchantments, and *which is known by the name of Weird-songs, but no such women came forward. Then was search made throughout the homestead if any woman were so learned.*

Then answered Gudrid, "I am not skilled in deep learning, nor am I a wise-woman, although Halldis, my foster-mother, taught me, in Iceland, the lore which she called Weird-songs."

"Then art thou wise in good season," answered Thorbjorg; but Gudrid replied, "That lore and the ceremony are of such a kind, that I purpose to be of no assistance therein, because I am a Christian woman."

Then answered Thorbjorg, "Thou mightest perchance afford thy help to the men in this company, and yet be none the worse woman than thou wast before; but to Thorkell give I charge to provide here the things that are needful."

Thorkell thereupon urged Gudrid to consent, and she yielded to his wishes. The women formed a ring round about, and Thorbjorg ascended the scaffold and the seat prepared for her enchantments. Then sang Gudrid the weird-song in so beautiful and excellent a manner, that to no one there did it seem that he had ever before heard the song in voice so beautiful as now.

The spae-queen thanked her for the song. "Many spirits," said she, "have been present under its charm, and were pleased to listen to the song, who before would turn away from us, and grant us no such homage. And now are many things clear to me which before were hidden both from me and others. And I am able this to say (Sephton, 1880).

It is still debated how one would reconstruct the practice based on that passage but generally modern Seidhr practitioners will use a special seat or chair and then cover their faces in some way, often using a veil, before using drumming or chanting to go into a trance. The seer then relays information gained from spirits, usually about things in the immediate future or answers to questions. Some also feel the use of a staff is helpful based on this passage and grave-finds of women buried with what are perceived to be magical paraphernalia including a special staff or rod; I have seen this used in oracular seidhr sessions where the seer slowly bangs the end of the staff on the ground to create a drum-like effect. The cat-skin gloves mentioned in the passage are probably significant and tied to Freya, possessor of cats, but that is not something incorporated into modern practice. It is possibly that the blud cloak is mean to relate to the dead, symbolized by the colour blue in older belief, and the feather pillow may echo Freya's feather cloak and connect the seer to the ability to shapeshift or travel outwards (Ward, 2022).

An adjacent practice which was not only used by seidhr practitioners but also by poets and lawgivers – so more accepted for men than seidhr work in general – was going under the cloak. This was used to foretell future events or to receive answers to questions and famously appears in Iceland during the conversion period where civil war was avoided by a law speaker going under the cloak to find a peaceful solution to the growing tensions between Norse pagans and Christians. The process was for the person to go somewhere they could be alone, lie down under a blanket or cloak which at least partially covered their face, go into a trance, and when ready return with the necessary information (Ward, 2022).

A related form of this type of seidhr practice is utiseta, literally 'sitting out', which is done to contact the spirits of the dead by sitting out on a grave or mound wrapped in a cloak. Utiseta in the lore could be very dangerous but could also offer many rewards, especially through new knowledge and prophecy, which the Norse believed could be given by the dead. The idea here was that by going under the cloak on a grave mound a person could contact the dead there and get answers from them; while this risked angering the dead and opened the person up to attack by them, the dead were understood to be more knowledgeable than the living and able to offer good counsel if they chose to (Ward, 2022). It is worth pointing out here that the threat from the dead isn't what modern readers might imagine, but it was believed that they could physically attack the living person or drive them mad (Adalsteinsson, 1978).

Another Seidhr practice is called sjonhverfing, literally "deceiving of the sight", where the practitioner makes others see or perceive what they want them to instead of what is really there. An example of this type of Seidhr magic is seen in Eyrbyggja Saga where a Seidhr worker named Katla tries to save her son from men intent on killing him. When the men come to Katla's house she hides him three times by telling him to remain completely still as she works her magic; each time the men see something different in the place of her son until they finally return with a Seidhr worker of their own. This form of magic is understood by some as a manipulation of the mind and by others as an actual illusion, which in either case creates the effect of disguising the target person or object. The implication in Eyrbyggja Saga was that it was a mental confusion that could be created magically rather than a real illusion, however, as Katla fails in the end when her head is covered by a bag and she is unable to continue influencing the men around her.

Katla's head being covered at the end of that story may relate to another aspect of Seidhr, the evil eye or ability to give a person bad luck by looking at them. Covering the Seidhr worker's head was seen as a protective measure (Ward, 2022). In several accounts of active Seidhr magic it's clear that the worker did need to see an object or person to effect it so the idea of blocking that ability is logical.

Seidhr, as with more commonly known Western European witchcraft, was also thought to be able to influence male potency. A Seidhr worker might cause impotence through sympathetic magic or otherwise curse a man so that he couldn't engage in intercourse with a woman he desired (Ward, 2022). This may offer another interesting potential tie in to Freya who has wider associations with both fertility and sex across her own folklore, making it rather logical that a magic taught by a Vanic deity should be able to impact things that were the purviews of the Vanir.

A final aspect of seidhr which clearly relates to Freya's stories is the belief that practitioners could shapeshift or could send their spirit out into an animal to possess its body for a period of time. The animals chosen – either in form or physically – were either sea mammals or animals related to Freya, including cats, pigs, and falcons (Ward, 2022). As with beliefs found across Europe such shapeshifting was thought to be a risk to the person doing it, and it was believed that to be harmed in spirit while out of one's body would cause real physical harm to the person even sometimes resulting in death.

This is only a brief summary of what Seidhr is and some aspects of Seidhr work but hopefully it is enough to help the reader better understand the concept and Freya's connection to it. Attempts to reconstruct the practice have been going on for decades and have had good results across the modern community although modern Seidhr, like its historic predecessor, can be considered controversial by some Heathens.

Freya in My Life

I learned the most about Freya and grew the closest to her in my personal practice during the period in which I was learning to practice seidhr. Seidhr as it is done today is a reconstructed practice and how it is practiced varies greatly from person to person or group to group. While everyone is working from the same source material the conclusions that are reached about methods and technique can be very different. This is just how I personally approach the subject and my connection to Freya through it.

Any type of seidhr work, to me, involves some level of trance work and so needs to be done carefully and with protection. That may mean different things for different people and groups; to me it means warding the space when doing deeper work, especially oracular work, and having allies to watch my back. I was dedicated to Odin,[20] who knows seidhr work, and I have a shrine to Freya, who they say was the first to teach seidhr to the Aesir. Before any planned working I offer to them both. I offer to my ancestors and to other particular spirits I work with when doing this type of work

Now things like weather work and shapeshifting I generally do when I am alone; it was common in both traditional seidhr for the person working to withdraw to a quiet place alone and lay or sit with their head covered. In seidhr work this is called going under the cloak and was also used by skalds (poets); it is a type of meditation that can be used for a variety of purposes from spellcasting, spirit journeying, to contacting spirits and receiving prophecies and poetic inspiration. I have found that even putting my hands over my eyes is effective for entering a trance. Influencing the weather is not my forte, and although I've had success, it takes a lot of energy and concentration and is usually done in a lighter trance. It involves, for me, going to where I want the change to manifest and then visualizing that change for as long as I can. It is a very tiring thing to do though and I have only ever focused on very slight changes in localized areas. Calling storms is a seidhr practice that I have never done, although I have diverted the damage of a storm around my home.

Shapeshifting can occur in any level of awareness, but I find I use it most often when my spirit is journeying outside my body. Such travelling, at least in human shape, seems to be common in modern seidhr, especially oracular work as many groups use a method where they journey to the gates of Hel or to the Well of Wyrd to answer questions. I haven't seen similar accounts in the lore, accept in the case of one story where a man sent his spirit in the form of a bear to fight against some other men – the bear disappeared when the man was awakened from his trance. However, in my opinion, this is an aspect that does lend itself to feeling closer to Freya as she was known to have her falcon cloak which allowed for transformations. Playing around with this in visualizations and journeywork has helped me work towards a stronger relationship with Freya because this type of spirit transformation is something I strongly associate with her.

When alone or with my own group I tend to use this travelling method to go and find answers. Now, my personal preference for a public oracular method is different, based on what I have reconstructed from the story of the seidhr worker in Eric the Red's Saga. I sit in a seat before the gathered people, with my face covered, and in my mind, I recite a chant I have written to call any goodly inclined, helpful spirits to me to answer the questions that will be asked. This does involve going into a deeper trance and after the session I will not remember anything that was said, by myself or others, although, so far, the results have been very good. I do not personally use drumming, although I can work and have worked with someone using drumming; it's just not something that I need. Most of what I do at this point is the result of years of trial and error learning and it is still evolving as I learn new methods.

Chapter 5

Freya in the Modern World

Freya is a popular deity and that is as true today as it was historically. We can find Freya in modern fiction, music, artwork, and in the worship and devotion of modern practitioners. She is a being who exists across folklore and spirituality but also across popular culture and mass media. Or put another way, Freya is as present in the world today as she was 100 years ago, although her form and stories may be different. This speaks to Freya's staying power across the centuries and the way that she still speaks to the creative imagination even in a secular world. And finding her in that world offers us a place to begin seeking her beyond the older sources.

A Note on A Difficult Subject

As we get into discussing Freya in the modern world, we need to take a moment first to address one problematic aspect of modern Heathenry, and by extension an issue that will impact anyone seeking to understand or connect to Norse gods: white supremacy. I would love to be able to write about Freya and not have to offer this caveat to readers, but unfortunately that's not an option because you all should be aware of this going in and also aware of things to avoid and watch out for. Freya is a beloved goddess and one who has a strong modern following; Heathenry – whether known as that or by specific tradition names – is a growing spiritual movement. And almost since the beginning of the revival of this spirituality, Heathenry has been shadowed by the dark history of the Nazi interest in the Norse gods and culture, which has created a modern movement based on those ideals. This is a problem for those seeking to connect to the Norse gods because racism and supremacy are not always, and especially initially, blatant or obvious. There are many code words and terms, referred to as dog whistles,[21] that are used to signal these ideas which can appear innocent without context but which are embedded with deeper and more problematic ideas. There are also entire groups that espouse ideas connected to white supremacy and segregation of spiritual practice based on ancestry, or more often based on superficial appearances, suggesting that the Norse gods only respond to or care about those with genetic roots in lands where they were worshipped. This, of course, overlooks the actual history of those places which never held any kind of genetic purity as a factor and of the mythology which doesn't in anyway support such ideas.

Many people seek spirituality by looking to their own heritage and there is nothing wrong with that, but that heritage is not in any way a prerequisite to Norse paganism or an interest in Freya. There is, and should be, no proof of ancestry required, no judgment based on appearance, no need to justify your interest. The world is an ever-changing place and diversity is a strength, not a weakness. If your ancestral connection does matter to you then seek to nourish and expand that, certainly, but never fall into the trap of seeing it as necessary to who and what you worship in a Norse context or the idea that humans can or should control who honours the Norse gods.

That all said, let's move on to places we can find Freya in the modern world.

Music

Wagner's Ring Cycle opera features a character named Freia who is a combination of Freya and Idunn.

Jethro Tull's song *Hunt By Numbers* refers to a cat as Freya's familiar.

Scarlet Letters has a song titled *Freya* which describes her as a goddess of war and mentions several points of her mythology in the lyrics.

Given the popularity of Norse mythology in heavy metal it's inevitable that there will be a wide array of various types of metal bands that mention or focus on Freya in their songs. I am including only a small sample here. The US heavy metal band The Sword has a song titled *Freya* about the goddess and some Norse mythology which was released as a single and appeared in the Guitar Hero II game. Canadian metal band Ashes of Yggdrasil has a song *In The Field of the Dead* which references Freya. The Norwegian metal band Enslaved has a song called *Sacrifice to the Elves* which mentions Freya.

Fiction

Freya appears in several different novels across the years, sometimes more or less like the Norse goddess and sometimes clearly only inspired by her. This list is a selection of these appearances to give readers an idea of the range involved.

Brisingamen by Diana Paxson – a grad student at Berkley finds Freya's necklace Brisingamen and channels Freya's power – and Freya – through it.

Runemarks by Joanne Harris – a story about a post-apocalyptic/ post Ragnarok world. Freya appears as a more minor character in the wider story, a shadow of the former goddess who has a serious grudge against Loki.

Claimed by Gods, by Eva Chase – is a romance series which features Freya as a secondary character.

Blue Moon, by Isobel Bird – the 6th book in the *Circle of Three* young adult series has Freya appear as a force which influences a young witch after being invoked on the full moon.

Magnus Chase (series) by Rick Riordan – Freya is a minor but repeating character. The mythology as presented in the series about Freya is mostly in line with Norse myths although she is presented as Freyr's twin sister and described in the modern stereotypical fashion: blond and blue eyed.

Odd and the Frist Giants, by Neil Gaiman – features Freya as a character. The book is a loose retelling of Norse myth.

Video Games

As with the other Norse deities Freya can be found, at least by name and general description, in several different video games.
Age of Mythology, 2002, allows players to choose Freya as a goddess to worship.
God of War, 2018, Freya is an ambivalent character that can help or hinder the player.
Smite, 2014, Freya is a playable character

Television

Freya is referenced in an episode of *Xena: Warrior Princess* where a sacrifice is to be made to the goddess.

In the third season of *The Last Kingdom,* Freya is prayed to by one of the characters, and similarly is referenced on the show *Vikings*.

The Norwegian television show *Ragnarök* includes a character based on the goddess Freya as does the Australian show *The Almighty Johnsons*. Both shows share the premise of Norse gods reincarnated into modern 21st century lives, with the humans embodying the gods on earth.

Comics

Freya does appear in the Marvel comics Thor series, although she is a bit obscure there and given a seemingly minor role. Some hints of the actual mythology occasionally shine through, such as a story where Loki borrows her falcon cloak, but by and large as with the rest of Marvel's Norse material it is heavily rewritten or modified; for example placing her as Freyr's daughter.

Envisioning Freya

One of the most basic aspects of understanding Freya may be how we visualize her. Our Gods, after all, have a concreteness to them that lends itself to imagery and they appear as active beings throughout the stories. We have myth, folklore, and ancient pagan artwork to pull from as we seek to imagine what our gods look like, although this often gives us little more than hints. We also have modern popular views, those ideas that come to us through artwork and mass media and which often influence us more strongly than we realize. These sources are invaluable, yet they can also be a double-edged sword; it may produce an accurate result, but it also complicates inspiration and emotion. For example even though we have no physical descriptions of Freya from the mythology beyond 'beautiful' and 'fair'[22] it is fairly common for people to depict and describe her as blonde and blue eyed, so much so that it is nearly a trope and is often simply assumed to be from the older source material.

The Freya that is found across most fiction will fit a similar pattern: tall, thin, beautiful, blond. In only a few cases, such as the depiction on the television show *Ragnarök*, does this vary. When a selection of modern heathens were surveyed in the book *Freya, Lady, Vanadis* they generally described Freya as *"blond, red haired, strawberry blond... Her eyes being perceived as blue, green, or grey."* (Lafayllve, 2006, p 68-69). This is in line with the wider cultural depictions of Freya across the last hundred years, from Arthur Rackham's 1910 illustration of Freya (found on the cover of this book) to the blond Freya of the Marvel comics. The culture around us has long shaped how we see Freya.

For myself at least, when I envision my Gods, I inevitably think of all these sources in an effort to come up with a correct image, but I'm aware that even the idea of having a correct image can be limiting. I am trying to take a lesson from my children now in this. There is a purity to the way that children approach the Gods that adults lose somewhere along the way. My oldest child, very unapologetically, has favourite Gods and they showed up in her artwork from time to time when she was younger. I have a drawing that she did of Freya when she was seven; it shows the Goddess as my child imagined her. This is Freya from the heart, without any worry of accuracy or careful details from the lore, and without the wider cultural impression of what Freya is supposed to look like. It's Freya as my daughter sees her without the filter we adults use for everything – with golden brown hair and a pink strapless dress. There is a beautiful purity to that, even if most other people wouldn't recognize the Freya in the image.

It's important to look to the body of myth and belief when we relate to deity, but it is just as important to listen to our hearts. I know that I tend to let my head complicate everything which is why I am trying to find a more balanced approach. Instead of rejecting the little things that pop up in my head – Odin with a hip flask, Freya with a butterfly tattoo – I'm going to try embracing them. I'm going to let my inner voice have its say and see what it comes up with. I may even grab some crayons and have a bit of fun with this. Even if the results are images that have no meaning to anyone but me, I am going to let my inner child have its say. It is so easy to ignore our inner voice when we feel like there is a right and wrong to what we are doing, but that inner voice can add a richness that is lacking in cold hard facts.

When you picture your Gods, how do you see them? As you imagine Freya how do you picture her?

Freya is a force in the world, and just as much so now as she was in the pre-Christian period. For those seeking to understand Freya it may seem odd to look to heavy metal or popculture television but all of these sources contribute to the wider cultural understandings of Freya and also often subconsciously influence how we personally relate to her. Seeking her out in the modern world is just as valuable in its own way is seeking her out in the older source material and helps us understand that she is present today in a very real way.

Freya In My Life

As much as I may talk about ways that we can intentionally seek to include Freya in our lives by building and creating things – whether that means poems or altars – there is also something to be said for the simple primal connection that we can nurture just by wanting to focus on her. The older material, the Eddas and Sagas, are great sources to start with in exploring who Freya is but it's important to also understand the value in newer stories and modern media where Freya can be found. She is pervasive. Even when the depictions are less than accurate, are caricatures, or stray wildly from the Norse goddess they still represent Freya's presence in the world. They can work to lead people to her older stories as well as her modern worship, if that is something a person is seeking.

One of my earliest encounters with Freya in modern media was through the 2001 young adult novel *Blue Moon* by Isobel Bird. In this story Freya appears as a goddess that is channelled by one of the main characters, causing the teenage girl to take on aspects of Freya's personality. Of course, things go sideways for the characters rather quickly in a way that offers a valuable life lesson about staying true to yourself, and Freya as she is shown through this process isn't a great deal like the actual Norse goddess – rather she's depicted as frivolous and focused on appearances. Nonetheless seeing Freya in this context and as a being who was tangibly real and able to influence humans was something I enjoyed and was refreshing in the context of the time the book was published. It made Freya *feel* modern to me at a time when I was struggling to see her as anything but a distant divine power and it helped me connect to her as something immanent instead of just figurative.

Chapter 6

Connecting to Freya Today

Having gotten this far in the book I hope we've established that Freya has a long and powerful history across Germanic spirituality and that she remains active in the world today, still acknowledged and honoured by many people. For those who choose to, you can move forward from here to begin actively connecting to Freya in as many ways, or as few, as you find comfortable. There is no right or wrong way to do this – despite what some people will definitely tell you – and I've always found it best to trust yourself in deciding when you are ready to take a new step. I'd also point out here before we go further that this sort of connection is highly personal and can't be measured or judged by others; there is no passing or failing.

I've found that people trying to nurture connections to the divine can put a lot of pressure on themselves to do so quickly or to do so in ways that look like what they see other people doing. But relationships with a goddess, like with a human, are always going to be unique and personal and never fit comfortably into a mould. You may find that you quickly connect to Freya – you may even realize that you were feeling her presence before you even started researching her – or you may find that despite a strong interest in her you feel absolutely no deeper connection. And that's all perfectly fine and normal. Sometimes the gods seek us out before we even know they're there and sometimes they don't respond no matter how much effort we put in to seeking them. As you move forward from here, if you choose to, embrace this as an organic process and accept it for what it is, no matter how it unfolds.

As we move into talking about active connection, I do want to briefly talk about UPG, a common term in modern Heathenry which is usually given as either unverified personal gnosis or unsubstantiated personal gnosis; my personal preference is to simply say personal gnosis. The idea with UPG is that it is knowledge of a deity (or spiritual subject) that has been gained through direct spiritual experience, dreams, visions, or similar personal sources and which can't be verified in older material (if it can be verified in the lore it's not UPG). UPG is sometimes looked down on or treated poorly as many people prefer clear historic precedent and citable sources for beliefs and practices relating to Norse gods, however, UPG does have its place and represents the lived, experiential side of modern heathenry. While we can and should look to the sources that we have to help build a connection to Freya – if we are seeking one – ultimately personal gnosis will come into play as we seek to nourish that connection and to establish our own understanding of Freya. Details like what she looks like, and hence what art best represents her, what offerings she prefers, how to know if she is pleased with an offering, are all things that develop through personal gnosis and learning to trust our own instincts and opinions about matters that otherwise have no clear answers.

There is also a related concept, sometimes called shared personal gnosis (SPG) or group gnosis that occurs when different people find they have the same experiences or ideas about a deity without having known each other before hand. This sort of community gnosis is the foundation for wider beliefs and occurs naturally over time.

Now, from here we can look at some more tangible methods of creating a connection. These will work with any deity but are focused on Freya and tailored to her particular mythology and wider beliefs about her. The idea is to use one or more of these things to help bring Freya into your own life, but as always remember that all you really need is a willingness to be open to her. The items and objects are helpful and fun but they are only external tools to create an internal connection.

Statues

In my opinion when selecting a statue for yourself you should consider two factors: what statue is going to work with your space and what statue appeals to you aesthetically. As with so many other things here there isn't any right or wrong and since the statue is supposed to be a tool to help you connect to the deity you want one that makes you think of Freya. Bigger isn't necessarily better and neither is any specific material, although an argument can be made for natural materials when possible. Beyond that the key is to find something that speaks to you personally and which you feel will help you create that connection to Freya. There are several statues of Freya on the market that you could choose from or you can find any statue that speaks to you with Freya's voice (figuratively) or even make your own.

Dryad Design offers three different options for statues of Freya as well as several jewellery pieces. They were all originally hand craved by artist Paul Borda based on details from Norse mythology, then cast in resin and the detail carries through.

Sacred Source has two statues of Freya and two plaques. These are museum replica pieces based on Norse art styles which may appeal to people who prefer a more historic look to their altar pieces.

There is also a wholesaling company that makes a more dramatic statue, styled after idealized Viking imagery, that can be found in many retailers who carry deity statues. They are more dramatic pieces and the aesthetic is a bit 'Hollywood'.

If none of these suit your taste there are a variety of hand carved or moulded options on sites like Etsy that can be made to order, although I do advise caution and some research before purchasing direct from artists; some are known to have ties to white supremacy groups.

Altars and Shrines

A main way to begin connecting to any deity or being is to set aside space for that deity in your life. This can be done in innumerable ways, from the very simple to the very complex, but most people choose either to build an altar or a shrine. There is, ultimately, a very fine line of difference between the two but we could say that an altar is a working space where a deity is honoured and offered to and religious rituals may be conducted, while a shrine is a space for a deity that is maintained for more personal devotion or practices. In other words an altar is an active space and a shrine is a more passive one, although again these concepts are loose and somewhat interchangeable.

To set up an altar to Freya you could use a statue or picture that reminds you of her or of something connected to her. As mentioned above there are many good options out there for statues in a variety of sizes and materials. If you don't like the idea of a statue, you could use a picture, either artwork depicting Freya (there is a huge amount to choose from) or any other image that reminds you of her, like a falcon, cats, or even a beautiful landscape image if it speaks to you. Because of her strong associations with gold and amber another option would be to include those as altar items to represent Freya. I know several people who use strands of amber or amber necklaces as a symbolic representation of Brisingamen on their altars, for example, and I have in the past used a small bottle of gold flakes as a stand in for Freya on a travel altar.

Other items kept on the shrine or altar will depend a lot on you and your personal faith tradition but at the most basic an offering bowl or plate is necessary. This is used in both more complex religious rituals as well as personal devotional rites, as the Norse put a lot of emphasis on reciprocity and giving gifts back to the gods in exchange for those we feel we are being given. There is no set style or type of offering bowl so this is another area where you can go with what you feel works best for you.

If you decide on an indoor space the first decision is whether it will be temporary or permanent. A temporary space can be set up and taken down again as needed while a permanent space would, of course, be there whenever its needed. The actual amount of space you need depends entirely on you and how big you want to make the shrine or altar. You can make use of a very small space with just a statue, candle, and bowl with everything sized to fit the area; I've seen museum replica Freya statues small enough to fit on a keychain that can be used for this purpose. I've also seen people use framed artwork of Freya over a small table which held an offering bowl, which wasn't an obvious shrine to anyone unfamiliar with pagan practices but definitely got the job done. You can also be as subtle as you like – there's no rule saying an altar or shrine has to loudly advertise what it is if you live in a religiously diverse household or just prefer not to draw attention to it. It's your spiritual area it should make you feel comfortable. That all said you can also go as big and elaborate with it as you like if that's what you want to do.

For an outdoor shrine or altar you want to find a space that is reasonably private and secluded. Beyond that, much like an indoor shrine, you can tailor the space to what suits you and make it as simple or detailed as you would like. I have seen outdoor shrines that are heavily decorated and complex and those that are nothing but a place for offerings next to a tree. The most important thing to remember in creating an outdoor space is that it will have to be able to hold up to whatever weather you get throughout the year, and you will need to be able to maintain it appropriately. If you want to have a statue outdoors you might want to find a stone statue or a resin image that's designed for outdoor use, carve something from wood, or use a natural object to represent Freya. One of the most beautiful outdoor shrine spaces to the Norse gods that I have personally seen is at Brushwood in New York and featured carved images that were out in a small clearing along with a small shrine area; my own outdoor home shrine is a stone offering space in front of a large tree where the tree, for me, represents the World Tree.

Offerings

A key aspect of Norse practice is the idea of offerings, with the belief that we give to the gods in exchange for what we get from them. When working with or honouring any Norse deity I think offerings are essential, although when, how often, and where to give them is up to personal preference. There are a variety of things that people may choose to offer to Freya based on both older beliefs and modern practices so I'll list a selection of options below.

Apples – it is mentioned as an older Swedish belief that Freya might visit orchards to bless them and so people would leave a few apples on the trees for her (Schön, 2004). In light of this I'd suggest that apples could be a good choice of offering for her, particularly in winter.

Pork – pork was a common ritual offering and meal and would be logical for Freya with her associations with pigs.

Strawberries – obviously not found in older folklore but it has become a rather common modern idea that Freya likes strawberries. This began, I believe, as personal gnosis but has become shared gnosis or community based belief.

Mead – an alcoholic drink made from honey would be a suitable offering to Freya.

Chocolate – mentioned as a suitable offering in *Our Troth* volume 1, like strawberries this is a modern shared gnosis.

To make an offering you would either pour it out, if it's a liquid, or leave it out, if its food item, while saying a few words about who it's for and why you are offering it. If you are doing this outdoors, please be mindful of the impact that what you are offering can have on the environment and animals.

Besides these tangible offerings there are some other options as well. You may choose to offer Freya an act of service by engaging in an activity you feel is associated with her or making a donation to charity in her name. You could sing a song or write a poem as an offering to her, or create a piece of art; I have in the past both written poems and drawn things which I then burned as offerings, so that the only copy was given fully to the gods. Your only limitation here is your own creativity.

Prayers and Poetry

I am a firm believer in the importance of prayer and poetry to both understand the gods and to help connect to them. We do have evidence of pre-Christian Norse peoples praying but we don't have many preserved examples of those prayers so what will be presented here is my own original work. I encourage readers to write their own as well, both as an exercise of devotion to Freya and as a way to actively participate in the process of connection to her. Remember these poems and prayers don't have to be perfect they just have to speak to you on a personal level.

Invocation to Freya
Freya
Vanadis
Powerful lady
We call to you

Freya
Gefn
Gift giver
We call to you
Freya
Mardoll
Sea bright
We call to you

Prayer to Freya for Prosperity

Freya, mother of treasure
We ask your blessing
May we have abundance
May our fortunes be fertile
May we succeed in all things
Bless us, Freya,
As we offer to you

In Praise of Freya

Golden teared goddess
Beautiful Vanir
Lady of magic
Freya
Boar rider
Falcon flyer
Cat driver
Freya
We praise your gifts
Abundant and joyous
Which bring life
And hope to all

Freya – a poem

Beautiful goddess

Goddess of love
Love of life
Life giving power
Power to transform
Transform tears
Tears to gold
Golden treasure
Treasure so beautiful
Beautiful goddess

Seidhr – A poem
My spirit moves
Inside my skin
Seething, seething, seething
Breaks free, bursting
Out beyond flesh
Shifting, shifting, shifting
My shape changing
Wearing wings, wild
Soaring, soaring, soaring
Clothed in feathers
Clothed in light
Straining, straining, straining
Down to the roots
Of the tree, of the world
Searching, searching, searching
Questions echoing
Answers waiting
Seeing, seeing, seeing

Guided Meditation to Freya

Another good way to begin to get to know a deity if you are more esoteric minded is with guided meditations or journeywork. This isn't for everyone, nor will the idea appeal to everyone but

I'd like to offer it here for those who do find this method helpful. For that reason I am including a simple guided meditation here for people to connect further to Freya. I would suggest either memorizing the text if you are doing this alone or pre-recoding it being read so you can play it back to use it.

Experiences and interactions during this should be treated as if they are as real as anything in the waking world and I encourage people to journal their experiences immediately afterwards. Be careful what you say or agree to as oaths carry as much weight in meditations as if in ritual, and oaths should be taken very seriously.

Sit comfortably somewhere that you won't be disturbed. Close your eyes. Take several slow, deep breaths. In your mind count down slowly from 10 as you imagine yourself surrounded by white light.

See yourself walking down a sunlit path through the woods. It is spring and you are surrounded by trees, their branches just starting to fill with bright green leaves. The sun shines down filtering through the leaves onto the dirt path you are walking on. As you walk the trees around you begin to thin and you step out into a clearing in the woods. The woods around you are full of bird song but the clearing is still and waiting.

After a moment Freya emerges from the far side. Take some time to study her as she walks out of the trees. What is she wearing? How does she look to you? How does the energy around her feel? She approaches you and greets you, telling you who she is and welcoming you to this place. If you have any questions now is the time to ask, otherwise you can simply listen to whatever she has to say to you. She may have personal messages or insights for you or she may have more general things to say. Take as long as you need for this conversation, but be sure to thank her when you feel you are finished.

When Freya leaves turn and go back down the path. Go back through the tunnel of trees. The trees around you grow denser and fuller as you walk deeper into the forest. The light dims.

Count up from ten. Take several slow, deep breathes. Feel your spirit settling fully back into your body. Wiggle your toes and fingers. Stretch slowly.

Open your eyes when you are ready.

You can repeat this meditation as often as you'd like, although you may find that Freya doesn't appear every time or that the results you get aren't always the same.

Ritual Bath

Another option for connecting to Freya could be a ritual bath where you use the time to focus on Freya and try to connect to her. Freya is a deity that is often associated with treasure in the older sources and with pleasure in modern ones so I think that something we may consider luxurious today – a nice soaking bath – can be an effective way to feel closer to her. If a bath isn't possible a shower is also an option or modifying this idea any other way you think might work for you. What follows is only my suggestion for what to do but feel free to adapt however you like: make it fancier or simpler as it pleases you. Remember the point here is for you to nurture this connection in a way that works for you.

Run a warm bath. Add sea salt and rose oil to the water as you prefer. Sit in the water and relax, allowing yourself to think of Freya. Don't question the thoughts that come up but allow them to come as they will. Give yourself time in this space to focus your full attention of Freya, who she is to you, what you think about her.

When you are finished get up and drain the water. Don't rush. Allow yourself to hold the relaxed contemplative air of the experience as long as possible. If you'd like to afterwards you can write down any particular thoughts or experiences you had.

Connecting to Freya is not a simple process or something that can be achieved quickly. You can focus on one of these suggestions or try several at once, or innovate your own ideas as you move forward. What matters isn't what you do, exactly, but that you are putting in the effort to do something.

Freya In My Life

By far my personal favourite image of Freya comes from Paul Borda of Dryad Designs. He offers three Freya statues, actually, but my favourite is the oldest, the standing Freya. She is depicted wearing her falcon cloak and Brisingamen, with her two cats near her side, a keyring and sword at her belt. The image is intricately carved, as are all of Borda's statues, and every detail of the image has meaning that ties into Freya's mythology and folklore. I appreciate these little details as well as a depiction of Freya that is, to me, sexual without being sexualized.

I have a small version of the statue (no longer in production) which I hand painted. I feel that the painting process helped me appreciate the details of the image more and also was a form of devotion to the goddess. Taking the time and effort to paint the image, choosing the colours, making sure it was done patiently and not rushed, all contributed to forming a deeper connection with Freya for me.

Conclusion

Freya is a complex goddess and this book, perhaps, begins to hint at some of the layers which she contains and which define her. She is strongly connected to other important powers within the Norse pantheon, including two of the three most popular pre-Christian gods: Odin and Freyr. She is the mother of 'treasure' both literally in the form of her daughter Hnoss and in the gold tears she cries, and figuratively in the gifts she gives to those who follow her. She is tied to every stage of human life, from conception, as a fertility goddess, through birth, as a deity possibly prayed to for a safe delivery, to death, as a goddess of the battle dead, at the least (Turville-Petre, 1964).[23] Her stories, while featuring a sexuality that can be difficult for modern mores to process, may have been more relatable to the pre-Christian Norse than the far more restrictive ethics that came into play later[24] (Simek, 2007). She is, ultimately, a goddess of human daily life who would have been understood as such by those who followed her.

In the 21st century, Freya is often pigeonholed into simple categories; a goddess of magic or of love or of beauty. She is reduced, too often, to her most pleasant aspects. But she is more than just a beautiful face or a bringer of love, more than just the 'Norse Venus'; she is a complex deity who can bring those pretty things but can also be hard to face. To understand Freya, fully understand her, we cannot shy away from the more difficult parts of her stories or try to ignore what we today may find unpleasant. She is a goddess who brought treasure and fertility and abundance, certainly. But she is also a goddess who turned her devoted follower and lover into a boar and rode him into Jotunheim, who made him earn in a tangible way the answers he was seeking. She is a goddess who claims half the battle dead for her own reasons. She is a goddess who taught seidhr – the good and the malevolent uses – to the Aesir and to humans. A goddess prayed to for a safe birth and connected with the dead who return to the land to fertilize it.

Freya's sexuality is embraced today in art and in stories, but usually the sanitized versions of it. She is praised as a goddess in control of her own body (which she was, clearly) without acknowledging that for her that meant taking any and all lovers she pleased. In our modern culture which still sees sexual openness as taboo and still chooses to put negative labels on women who are free with their sexual favours Freya's choosing to be with everyone she pleases, while married, is often an uncomfortable fact that's glossed over. We still live with a century and more of Freya's stories being turned into morality tales where she is shamed for her sexuality and choices. In 19th century Sweden a poet called prostitutes Freya's children[25] yet today we distance ourselves from the idea of sex work or its possible connection to a goddess or sacredness. Yet all of this is part of who Freya is, an unapologetically sexual goddess. The active aspect of fertility and love that is as bawdy and passionate as it is romantic. The primal sweat of sex as much as the caress of a lover.

Having come this far in this book, it may be worth stopping and thinking about what Freya and her stories makes you the most uncomfortable. What pieces of who Freya is do you have the hardest time looking at – and why? It is easy to love Freya for the beauty and the treasure, even the tears of gold, but if we seek to truly know her, we must look without flinching at every side of her. See the cats pulling her chariot not only as soft and appealing but also as dangerous killers. See Brisingamen as her symbol and her power but also as a thing which she was willing to earn for herself in a way that has been making commentators uncomfortable for centuries.

Freya is not a goddess to be taken in pieces or sanitized into acceptability; she is the full scope of life and death, the beautiful and the terrifying. She goes on her own terms or not at all.

Pronunciation Guide

I am caveating this section by saying that I am not a fluent speaker of Icelandic or old Norse and am offering here the pronunciations as I am aware of them for a selection of the words in this book. They do vary by language and dialect and, as with most things in modern Heathenry, practitioners of Norse spiritualities do not necessarily agree on how these should be pronounced. Nonetheless I think it is helpful for the reader to have at least a general idea. Any and all errors here are my own.

Aesir – Ay-seer (the main group of Norse gods)
Brisingamen – Brih-sihn-gah-mehn (Freya's necklace)
Freya – Fray-uh (old Norse froy-uh)
Freyr – Fray-uhr (sometimes also given as Frey)
Gefn – Geh-fn
Hnoss – H-nawss
Loki – low-key
Mardoll – Muhr-dawll
Njorð – Nyor-th
Odin – Oh-din (this definitely has multiple various pronunciations)
Oðr – Oth-r
Seidhr – sayth (a form of trance magic)
Spae – spay (a type of visionary practice)
Syr – Seer
Thor – Thore (with a th like in 'the')
Vanic – Van-ik
Vanir – Van-eer (the secondary group of Norse Gods, later included with the Aesir)
Volva – vul-vuh (term for a type of seeress)

Appendix A

Additional Resources

If you have found Freya interesting and would like to dig deeper into who she is you can look at the books in the bibliography for further reading. I would also like to include here some other resource options that might be helpful in a continuing quest to get to know this fascinating Vanic goddess.

Online resources

There is a collection of public domain copies of the Eddas and Sagas on the Sacred Texts website. These are good resources to begin with, especially if budget is an issue, but any translation that comes from that period must be read in its context: translators during the Victorian era tended to omit material they found inappropriate (based on their own mores) and to add material that they felt was either needed or made the story more interesting

The material can be found here http://www.sacred-texts. com/neu/ice/index.htm

'Freya' on 'Norse Mythology for Smart People' another site with an academic tone and solid references. This entry offers a good concise overview of who Freya is, although I will caution readers that the author supports the argument that Freya and Frigga are the same.

https://norse-mythology.org/gods-and-creatures/the-vanir-gods-and-goddesses/freya/

The Northvegr website is a good source for material on Norse culture in general

http://www.northvegr.net/

The Viking Answer Lady webpage discusses Freya in a few articles, including one on seidhr. It is also a good page in general to use as a resource for more specific questions.

http://www.vikinganswerlady.com/seidhr.shtml

Endnotes

1. There is supposition that she did, since her brother, Freyr, is known to also go by the name of Ingve, but unfortunately whereas Freyr's mythology under that personal name have survived Freya's, if she had any, has not.
2. Literally a female dog, although it is likely that the implication was also of sexual promiscuity.
3. It is heavily implied that Gullveig and Heidhr are also Vanic goddesses they are never explicitly named as such, and as will be discussed, may represent alternate names for Freya herself anyway.
4. I acknowledge that this is an unpleasant and possibly upsetting topic, however, it's impossible to discuss Freya or the Vanir in any actual depth without discussing the repeated sibling relationships that are referenced in their mythology and the implications of possible historic practices among human cultures. I will state as clearly as I can here that incest is seen as morally wrong today and no part of this book is meant to deny that or justify it. I am also in no way supporting Simek's assertion that incest is connected to matrilineal practices but feel it's important to relay his theories around the Vanic cult in their entirety.
5. Page 30 of *Gods and Myths of Northern Europe*.
6. Specifically the story of the rebuilding of the walls of Asgard, where Freya is one of the demands made by the builder as payment for his work. If Freya had already been taken among the Aesir before the peace hostages were exchanged it would explain her presence for that story, although it is equally possible that she came with her father and brother without being explicitly mentioned as a hostage. I would caution readers against looking for definitive answers here, as its worth remembering that

the material is often contradictory – for example we are told Njorð and Freyr came as peace hostages but also that Freyr and Freya were born after Njorð's failed marriage to Skadhi which occurs later.

7. Effectively a ritualized trading of insults between people.

8. Female members of the Aesir.

9. Thor's wife.

10. This story – or a version of it – may perhaps be found in later Orkney folklore which tells of two kings who battle each other throughout eternity and will find peace only at Ragnarök. http://www.orkneyjar.com/tradition/everlastingbattle.htm

11. It was said to be too passionate and potentially slanderous to the recipient.

12. Sex here is being discussed in a heteronormative context, and primarily as a means of reproduction tied to fertility, but it shouldn't be assumed that this would be Freya's only connection to the wider subject. I recommend Lafayllve, *Freya, Lady, Vanadis* Chapter 2 for a more in-depth discussion of the possible nuances to be found here.

13. It is worth noting that the loss of sun and moon and an endless winter are key aspects to the start of Ragnarök, the foretold final battle between the Aesir and giants.

14. Brising means flame or fire and is the name of a Dwarf.

15. If one can ever be said to own a cat.

16. I was told that this was a personal choice in an online correspondence with the author, however, it is also publicly referenced in *Our Troth,* volume 1, page 373.

17. This is implied but not explicitly stated in the source. Dr. Crawford suggests that it is also possible that folkvangir may be directly connected to Odin's place, Valhalla, and that the two may even be synonymous. The original source is unclear on the exact details.

18. If we assume that Freya is in fact also Heidhr.

19. I must, of course, note here that the use of the term shamanism outside very specific cultures from which the term originated is controversial.

20. I've also discussed my practice of seidhr in my book *Pagan Portals - Odin*.

21. A better explanation of this and list of common dog whistles you will find in Heathenry can be found online here: https://m.box.com/shared_item/https%3A%2F%2Fapp.box.com%2Fs%2Frfmafp0h7lbcybbi7vjfw8036m2867pd%3Ffbclid%3DIwAR0zGHG_III14n_GIM7-zs8vdQxatWpl7gIACQDG5oVt9mMoXAGEN4E9MOM?fbclid=IwAR1KVcLMEssNyq-MlPqTrxZ2RuYy94K3YiZn8AkMeio_LjO9aTKWhNsYCQA

22. I will as always caution readers not to assume too much from the modern English word fair. One would have to look at the original term in the original language to grasp what was being implied in the context the term was used and I have found that often it isn't what a modern English speaker might assume.

23. I am paraphrasing Turville-Petre and Simek here but it should be understood that his work is quite hostile to Freya and her sexuality which he goes out of his way to criticize throughout his text, despite his argument that she is a fertility goddess par excellence.

24. Simek is more neutral on Freya's sexuality and ties it into a Vanic fertility cult practiced by the 'common' people as opposed to nobility which Freya may have represented.

25. Noted in Schön, 2004.

Bibliography

Adalsteinsson, J., (1999). *Under the Cloak: a Pagan Ritual Turning Point in the Conversion of Iceland*

— (1998). *A Piece of Horse Liver: Myth, Ritual and Folklore in Old Icelandic Sources*

American Heritage Dictionary (n.d.) https://www.ahdictionary.com/word/indoeurop.html

Bauschatz, P., (1982). *The Well and the Tree*

Bellows, H., (1936). *The Poetic Edda*

Blain, J., (2002). *Nine Worlds of Seid-Magic*

Brodeur, A., (1916). *Prose Edda*

Byock, J., (1998). *The Saga of King Hralf Kraki*

— (2005). *The Prose Edda*

Crawford, J., (2022). *Fólkvangr*. Retrieved from https://www.youtube.com/watch?v=gMgOPhlwVk8

Crossley-Holland, K., (1980) The Norse Myths

Ellis, H., (1968). *The Road to Hel*

Ellis-Davidson, H., (1964). *Gods and Myths of Northern Europe*

— (1988). *Myths and Symbols in Pagan Europe*

— (1993). *The Lost Beliefs of Northern Europe*

Ewing, T., (2008). *Gods and Worshippers in the Viking and Germanic World*

Fortson, B., (2004). *Indo-European language and culture: an introduction*

Grimm, J., (1888). *Teutonic Mythology*, volume 1

Grundy, S., (1995). *The Cult of Odinn: God of Death?*

— (1994). *Miscellaneous Studies Towards the Cult of Odinn*

Guðmundsson, Ó., (2016). *Sex in the Sagas: Love and Lust in the Old Icelandic Literature*

Gundarsson, K., (2006). *Our Troth*, volume 1

Harper, D., (2022). Online Etymology Dictionary, 'Freya', retrieved from https://www.etymonline.com/word/freya

Heath, C., (2021). *Elves, Witches, and Gods: Spinning Old Heathen Magic in eth Modern Day*

Herbert, K., (1995). *Looking for the Lost gods of England*

Jones, M (2003). *The Wild Hunt*. Retrieved from www.maryjones. us/jce/wildhunt.html

Lafayllve, Patricia, (2006). *Freya, Lady, Vanadis: An Introduction to the Goddess*

Larrington, C., (1996). *The Poetic Edda*

Lindow, J., (2001). *Norse Mythology: a guide to the Gods, heroes, rituals and beliefs*

Näsström, B., (1995). *Freyja – the Great Goddess of the North*

North, R., (2010). *Eilífr Goðrúnarson, 'Eulogy on Þórr' (Þórsdrápa)* Retrieved from http://www.worldtreeproject.org/document/ 2288

O'Donoghue, H., (2008). *From Asgard to Valhalla*

Paxson, D., (1993). *Heide: Witch goddess of the North*. Retrieved from https://hrafnar.org/articles/dpaxson/asynjur/heide/

Pollington, S., (2003). *The Mead-Hall: Feasting in Anglo-Saxon England*

Scudder, B., (1997). *Egil's Saga*

Sephton, E., (1880). *The Saga of Erik the Red*. Retrieved from https://sagadb.org/eiriks_saga_rauda.en

Schön, E., (2004). *Asa-Tors hammare, Gudar och jättar i tro och tradition*

Scudder, B., (2001). *Egil's Saga*

Shipley, J., (1984). *The Origins of English Words*

Simek, R., (2007). *Dictionary of Northern Mythology*

Turville-Petre, E., (1964). *Myth and Religion of the North*

Vikis-Freibergs, V., (2007). *Amber in Latvian Folk Songs and Beliefs*. Retrieved from https://www.tandfonline.com/doi/ abs/10.1080/01629778500000221

Ward, C., (2022) *Women and Magic in the Sagas*. Retrieved from http://www.vikinganswerlady.com/seidhr.shtml

About the Author

Morgan Daimler is a blogger, poet, teacher of esoteric subjects, witch, and priestess of the Daoine Maithe. Morgan is a prolific pagan writer, having published more than a dozen books under Moon Books alone, and she is one of the world's foremost experts on all things Fairy. She lives in Connecticut, US.

SELECTED TITLES

Norse Mythology
Odin
Thor
The Norse

Fairy Lore
Fairies
Fairycraft
Aos Sidhe
Fairy Witchcraft
A New Dictionary of Fairies

Irish Mythology
Lugh
The Dagda
The Morrigan
Irish Paganism
Raven Goddess
Manannán mac Lir

You may also like

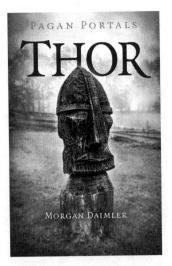

Thor by Morgan Daimler

Thor is an immensely popular God but also one of contradictions,
whose complexity is sometimes underrated. Often depicted as oafish,
he was clever enough to outwit the dwarf Alviss (All-wise). A god
of storms and thunder, he also brought fertility and blessed brides
at weddings. A defender of civilization and order against entropy
he usually travelled with a trickster deity. This basic introductory
book looks at the history and mythology of the Norse deity Thor,
untangling older beliefs from modern popculture.

978-1-78904-115-6 (Paperback)
978-1-78904-116-3 (ebook)

Bestsellers from Moon Books
Pagan Portals Series

The Morrigan
Meeting the Great Queens
Morgan Daimler
Ancient and enigmatic, the Morrigan reaches out to us.
On shadowed wings and in raven's call, meet the ancient Irish
goddess of war, battle, prophecy, death, sovereignty, and magic.
Paperback: 978-1-78279-833-0 ebook: 978-1-78279-834-7

The Awen Alone
Walking the Path of the Solitary Druid
Joanna van der Hoeven
An introductory guide for the solitary Druid, The Awen Alone will
accompany you as you explore, and seek out your own place
within the natural world.
Paperback: 978-1-78279-547-6 ebook: 978-1-78279-546-9

Moon Magic
Rachel Patterson
An introduction to working with the phases of the Moon,
what they are and how to live in harmony with the lunar
year and to utilise all the magical powers it provides.
Paperback: 978-1-78279-281-9 ebook: 978-1-78279-282-6

Hekate
A Devotional
Vivienne Moss
Hekate, Queen of Witches and the Shadow-Lands,
haunts the pages of this devotional bringing magic
and enchantment into your lives.
Paperback: 978-1-78535-161-7 ebook: 978-1-78535-162-4

Bestsellers from Moon Books
Shaman Pathways Series

The Druid Shaman
Exploring the Celtic Otherworld
Danu Forest
A practical guide to Celtic shamanism with exercises
and techniques as well as traditional lore for
exploring the Celtic Otherworld.
Paperback: 978-1-78099-615-8 ebook: 978-1-78099-616-5

The Celtic Chakras
Elen Sentier
Tread the British native shaman's path,
explore the goddess hidden in the ancient stories;
walk the Celtic chakra spiral labyrinth.
Paperback: 978-1-78099-506-9 ebook: 978-1-78099-507-6

Elen of the Ways
British Shamanism - Following the Deer Trods
Elen Sentier
British shamanism has largely been forgotten: the reindeer
goddess of the ancient Boreal forest is shrouded in mystery...
follow her deer-trods to rediscover her old ways.
Paperback: 978-1-78099-559-5 ebook: 978-1-78099-560-1

Deathwalking
Helping Them Cross the Bridge
Laura Perry
An anthology focusing on deathwalking and psychopomp work:
the shamanic practice of helping the deceased's soul pass on to
the next realm.
Paperback: 978-1-78535-818-0 ebook: 978-1-78535-819-7

Bestsellers from Moon Books

Keeping Her Keys
An Introduction to Hekate's Modern Witchcraft
Cyndi Brannen
*Blending Hekate, witchcraft and personal development together
to create a powerful new magickal perspective.*
Paperback: 978-1-78904-075-3 ebook 978-1-78904-076-0

Journey to the Dark Goddess
How to Return to Your Soul
Jane Meredith
*Discover the powerful secrets of the Dark Goddess and
transform your depression, grief and pain into healing
and integration.*
Paperback: 978-1-84694-677-6 ebook: 978-1-78099-223-5

Shamanic Reiki
Expanded Ways of Working with Universal Life Force Energy
Llyn Roberts, Robert Levy
*Shamanism and Reiki are each powerful ways of healing; together,
their power multiplies. Shamanic Reiki introduces techniques to
help healers and Reiki practitioners tap ancient healing wisdom.*
Paperback: 978-1-84694-037-8 ebook: 978-1-84694-650-9

Southern Cunning
Folkloric Witchcraft in the American South
Aaron Oberon
*Modern witchcraft with a Southern flair, this book is a
journey through the folklore of the American South and
a look at the power these stories hold for modern witches.*
Paperback: 978-1-78904-196-5 ebook: 978-1-78904-197-2

Readers of ebooks can buy or view any of these bestsellers by clicking on the live link in the title. Most titles are published in paperback and as an ebook. Paperbacks are available in traditional bookshops. Both print and ebook formats are available online.

Find more titles and sign up to our readers' newsletter
http://www.johnhuntpublishing.com/paganism

Follow us on Facebook
https://www.facebook.com/MoonBooks

Follow us on Instagram
https://www.instagram.com/moonbooksjhp/

Follow us on Twitter
https://twitter.com/MoonBooksJHP

Follow us on TikTok
https://www.tiktok.com/@moonbooksjhp